ATTENTION!

BAR CODE IS LOCATED
    INSIDE OF BOOK

ID0583253

**DO NOT REMOVE
CARDS FROM POCKET**

**ALLEN COUNTY PUBLIC LIBRARY
FORT WAYNE, INDIANA  46802**

You may return this book to any agency, branch,
or bookmobile of the Allen County Public Library.

DEMCO

*AMERICA AND THE*
*CIVIL WAR ERA 1850-1875*

# America and the
# Civil War Era 1850-1875

Fon W. Boardman, Jr.

HENRY Z. WALCK, INC.
A DIVISION OF
*David McKay Company, Inc.*
NEW YORK

**Library of Congress Cataloging in Publication Data**
Boardman, Fon Wyman, 1911-
    America and the Civil War era, 1850-1875.

    Bibliography: p.
    Includes index.
    SUMMARY: An overview of all aspects of life in
the United States before, during, and after the Civil War.
    1.   United States—History—1849-1877—Juvenile
literature.   [1.   United States—History—1849-1877]
I.   Title.
E415.7.B59          973.7          76-12231
ISBN 0-8098-5011-7

# Contents

1941848

# 1 From Compromise to Controversy

THE LONG debate, so bitter at times that many people feared the Union was about to split apart, was over. The result, the Compromise of 1850, consisted of five bills passed by Congress and signed into law in September by President Millard Fillmore. Only two months earlier, Fillmore had succeeded to the presidency when President Zachary Taylor died. The Compromise, most citizens hoped, settled once and for all what, in recent years, had become an increasingly acrimonious argument between North and South. At the root of the disturbing debate was the institution of black slavery.

Antislavery agitation in the North had increased in the 1840's. The South, in reaction, defended slavery more openly, both by word and deed. Meanwhile, the growing demand for cotton and the spread of its cultivation over larger areas of the South and Southwest fastened slavery as an economic system so firmly on the South that even some who would have liked to see it ended despaired of finding a practical way to do so. The escalating clash of interests and beliefs was further aggravated by the Mexican War, beginning in 1846. Many people in the North opposed the war, seeing it as an attempt by the South to conquer more slave territory. Before the war ended, Congress began to debate the issue of slavery in relation to the probable results of the war. By the treaty that ended the war in 1848, the United

*1*

States acquired from Mexico land that included all the later states of California, Nevada and Utah, almost all of New Mexico and Arizona, and parts of Colorado and Wyoming.

The more extreme southerners tried to use the occasion not only to make slavery legal in all this new territory, but also to write into law their conviction that Congress could not exclude slavery from any territory. Northern abolitionists, on the other hand, wanted to take the occasion to exclude slavery from all the territories forever. Congress, however, included among its leaders men who put the Union ahead of all else and who sought a compromise. Foremost among these was Senator Henry Clay (1777-1852) of Kentucky, who had served in Congress or the cabinet most of the time since 1806. He offered an eight-part bill that was the focal point of the debate that followed. The strongest voice among northern supporters of a compromise was that of the eloquent senator from Massachusetts, Daniel Webster (1782-1852), who had first been elected to Congress in 1813 and who, like Clay, had served in the cabinet. In what many consider the greatest speech ever delivered in the Senate, Webster, in March 1850, urged tolerance on both sides in order to preserve the Union.

In the end, the leading role in securing agreement on a compromise was played by a senator of a younger generation, Stephen A. Douglas (1813-61). Born in Vermont, Douglas went to Illinois as a young man and soon was successful both in law and in politics. Elected to the House of Representatives in 1843, he became a senator four years later and remained so until his death. Short and stocky, with dynamic movements of the body, and a loud voice that he enjoyed using, Douglas was known as "The Little Giant" and was one of the emerging leaders of the nation.

Congress eventually passed five bills, in the drafting of which Douglas played a major part. These bills admitted California as a free state; organized New Mexico and Utah as territories and gave the voters there the right to decide the slavery issue for themselves; granted Texas $10,000,000 for abandoning its claim to any New Mexican territory; abolished the slave trade in the District of Columbia, but not slavery itself; and amended the Fugitive Slave Act of 1793 to make it stronger.

Like most compromises, this one did not please everyone. The extreme abolitionists in the North refused to accept the new fugitive slave law. Prominent citizens, including Ralph Waldo Emerson, the leader of the intellectuals, openly advocated disobedience. Southern extremists, on the other hand, felt the South had given up far more than it should have. A Georgia newspaper editor warned ominously that the feud between the North and the South "may be smothered but never overcome." The Compromise weakened both the Democratic party and the Whig party because sectional differences now exerted a stronger pull on voters than did party ties. The Whigs, in fact, ceased to exist in a few years; the Democrats, as a party with an older tradition and more common interests apart from slavery, were somewhat better off. The majority of the people, both North and South, probably supported the Compromise because they wanted an end to threats and counterthreats.

Southern leaders made it clear that the Fugitive Slave Act was the key to the success or failure of the Compromise. Unless the North accepted both the letter and the spirit of the law, they said, the Compromise was dead. The very vocal abolitionists made it equally clear that they would not accept the law. Consequently, the Compromise led to renewed bad feeling and controversy almost as soon as it became law.

The act concerning fugitive slaves placed such cases under Federal jurisdiction and provided for the appointment of special commissioners who could issue warrants for the arrest of fugitives and who could also order them returned to their masters. Alleged fugitives were not allowed to testify on their own behalf, and anyone obstructing the law or helping fugitive slaves to escape could be fined $1,000 and sentenced to jail for six months. The commissioners received a fee of $10 when they allowed a slave to be returned to a master, but only $5 if they ruled against the alleged owner. Northern states, in the very year the Compromise was passed, began to enact or expand existing "personal liberty laws." Public attorneys in some states were charged with defending fugitives, while public buildings could not be used to detain them. Some states forbade any citizen to assist in any way in enforcing the law.

In the month the Compromise bills became law, an alleged fugitive slave was saved from deportation to the South when enough money was raised to buy his freedom. Before long, incidents were reported from Boston to Chicago and in many cases mobs, armed and ready to use violence if necessary, rescued blacks from the law. An owner was killed and his son wounded in Lancaster, Pennsylvania, when they attempted to recover two fugitives. In Syracuse, New York, in 1851, a group of men rescued a fugitive named Jerry from jail and sent him to Canada. A newspaper editor in Milwaukee, Wisconsin, was imprisoned in 1854 for organizing the rescue of a slave from jail. Perhaps the most spectacular rescue attempt, which failed, took place in Boston in 1854. The authorities had to assemble 1,100 armed men, including United States Marines, a regiment of artillery and Federal marshals, in order to hold off a mob and get one slave, Anthony Burns, on board a ship to be sent back to Virginia.

The United States of the 1850's, except for the controversy over slavery, was a generally contented nation of continuing, almost spectacular, growth in area, population and economic well-being. The admission of California in 1850 brought the number of states to thirty-one, sixteen of which were free and fifteen slave. Never again would the South be equal with the North in this respect, which meant the South was now in the minority in the Senate. By this time, too, the population of the North exceeded that of the South to such an extent that the former had 144 members of the House of Representatives as against ninety from the slave states.

The territorial dimensions of the United States out of which the forty-eight contiguous states were eventually established reached completion in 1853 with the Gadsden Purchase. This piece of Mexican territory, amounting to 30,000 square miles, later formed parts of New Mexico and Arizona. The nation's chief interest in the territory, for which it paid Mexico $10,000,000, was as part of a southern route for a proposed railroad to the Pacific. The purchase took its name from James Gadsden (1788-1858), a diplomat and railroad promoter from South Carolina, who was sent as minister to Mexico to negotiate the deal. The Senate ratified the treaty by only a narrow margin.

The census of 1850 reported a population of 23,191,876, an increase of slightly more than 6,000,000 since 1840. By 1860, the census showed a further increase of more than 8,000,000, to 31,443,321. The North and West held 20,309,960 persons; the South, 11,133,361. By this time, too, one of every seven persons was a black and one of seven was foreign born. The nation's population had passed that of the British Isles and was rapidly catching up with France and Germany.

Behind the statistics on territory, states and population lay some of the causes of friction between North and South—friction that stemmed from economics and from political philosophy rather than slavery. Many northern businessmen, especially those who had dealings with the cotton planters of the South, favored the Compromise of 1850 if for no other reason than that an end to agitation would be good for business. But the North in general looked upon the South as backward economically and feudal in its social structure. In terms of industrial development, finance and business, this was true. The North was rapidly becoming one of the world's leading centers of industrialism and all that that meant in related matters of large cities and an urban working class. At this same time, both the Old Northwest (the area between the Allegheny Mountains and the Mississippi and north of the Ohio River) and the Far West found their ties with the Northeast increasing at the expense of the South. As east-west transportation improved and as the eastern population needed more of the agricultural products of the West, that region became closely linked to the urban industrial centers. More of the West's products were going east by 1860 than down the Mississippi to New Orleans.

The North complained, with some justice, that the South dominated the Federal government out of proportion to its population and economic strength. Through 1852, nine of the thirteen presidents had been born in the South, while the two elected in 1852 and 1856, although northerners, were Democrats sympathetic to southern views. The president's cabinet usually had a majority of southerners in it, and the most important committee chairs in Congress seemed to be held continually by men from the same region. In addition, five of the nine justices of the Supreme Court were from the South. Northern business interests wanted protective tariffs on imported manufactured goods, along with internal improvements such as roads, canals and railroads built at the expense of the Federal government. The West wanted a law that would make it easier for settlers to acquire public land. The South opposed all of these.

The South was dominated politically and economically by the planter class and the professional classes, especially lawyers, aligned with them. Both these groups seemed more willing to devote their careers to government than did northerners and so they acquired seniority and position. Nevertheless, by the 1850's, southern leaders believed the North was trying to dominate it economically, as well as to confine, if not end, slavery. Although small farmers, poor whites and blacks together far outnumbered the planters and their allies, the popular image of the South was that of the plantation, with its gallant men and beautiful women, leading lives of leisure and chivalry. Many of the successful planters, as a matter of fact, were self-made men; few could claim the romantic cavalier background or ancestry that they copied. Even though the South's way of life ran counter to the trend of the times, southern leaders fought strenuously to stem that trend. They said too many southerners went north to college, that the textbooks used in southern schools were written in the North and that the South was too dependent on northern books, magazines and intellectual leadership in general.

Overshadowing all this, though, the main problems of the South were how to deal with the slave system, with blacks as a different race, and with the increasing clamor in the North for an end to slavery. There were 3,638,808 blacks in the United States in 1850, of whom 3,204,313 were slaves. By 1860 the total number of blacks was 4,441,830, and 3,953,760 were slaves. Thus by then about a third of the population of the slave states was black. As to ownership, though, only 385,000 whites owned slaves while about 1,500,000 southern families had no slaves at all. Most owners held fewer than ten slaves; only 107,957 owned more than ten, while only 1,733 owned more than 100. Of the slave population in 1850, 2,800,000 lived on farms or plantations and of these 1,800,000 were engaged in raising cotton. The other 400,000 lived mostly in cities and about 200,000 of them labored in industries such as tobacco factories and textile mills, or in lumbering and mining.

The slaves were entirely at the mercy of their owners so far as food, housing, clothing, medical care and punishment were concerned. The treatment of slaves varied, depending on the personality of the owner and the efficiency of the plantation. A slave owner had to take care of a slave from the cradle to the grave. This was no small obligation, but also meant that it was to the advantage of the owner to treat the slaves so as to get the maximum amount of work out of them. On plantations the usual housing was a log cabin, probably with a dirt floor and consisting of one or two rooms for a family. Food, a great deal of which consisted of pork and corn, was usually adequate and often slaves were allowed to raise vegetables and chickens. Clothing was cheap but adequate. A male slave would probably receive four shirts and four pairs of pants a year; a female slave, four dresses. Whipping was a universal form of punishment and its severity or frequency depended on the owner. Some slaves died of whippings, but most masters did not want to harm slaves in such a way as to impair their economic usefulness. No matter how well-treated a slave might be, however, the fact remained that he or she was a piece of property with no control over his or her life.

Slave owners were free at any time to sell their slaves and the domestic slave trade was an important part of the system. For about half a century before 1860, slavery spread south and west from the coastal states as planters sought new and fertile land, first in Alabama and Mississippi, then in Texas and Arkansas. Thousands of slaves accompanied their masters westward, while about 127,000 slaves were sold in the East and transported to the West in this half-century. Virginia, where soil exhaustion reduced the profitability of agriculture, was a leading supplier of slaves to the cotton plantations.

Since 1808 it had been illegal to import slaves into the United States. Now, in the 1850's, some southerners were agitating for the reopening of this trade to meet the demand caused by the continued increase in cotton production. Ships of the American and British navies patrolled the African slave coast, but not too effectively. Between 1843 and 1857, the Americans captured twenty-nine slavers, only six of which were condemned. The British, on the other hand, made nearly 600 seizures. During the 1850's the number of slaves brought into the country illegally ran into five figures. In two cases in 1858, when the navy captured slave ships, a jury in South Carolina and another in Georgia found the perpetrators not guilty. Some of the slave ships were fitted out in northern ports and made profits for northern shippers, although many of these ships were owned by Cuban or Brazilian interests.

Slavery's defenders contended that the blacks were well off and contented, but they lived in constant fear of slave revolts. Rumors of slave plots were common, although few materialized. What could have been a serious revolt in New Orleans, involving 2,500 slaves, was prevented in 1853 when a free Negro informed on the conspirators. In eastern North Carolina in 1860, a score of slaves, meeting in a swamp, planned an insurrection. They hoped to get several hundred more to join them, then to kill all the whites they could find, seize money and weapons and escape on a ship. Again the plotters were betrayed.

From the standpoint of economics, a slave was a piece of property and represented a capital investment on the part of the owner. The value of slaves fluctuated with economic conditions, and during the 1850's for the most part the demand was such that slave prices increased. The average value of a slave in 1860 was about $700, but a prime field hand—a young adult male— would bring up to $2,000.

Whether the slave system of agriculture was economically efficient and profitable to the plantation owners has been debated for many years. Most opinion now holds that it was profitable. Some plantations, of course, lost money in some years and with weather and the world price of cotton beyond the control of the planters, an efficiently run plantation might lose money, with or without slavery. Profits were greater in the fertile land of the Mississippi delta than in the southeast where the land had been cultivated longer.

Slavery was based in part on the assumption that the blacks were an inferior race, and even many persons opposed to slavery believed this. At best, they felt that slavery retarded such mental and moral development of the blacks as would be possible if they were free. When attacks on slavery became fiercer, southerners began to take a more positive position in their defense of it. Thanks to it, they said, the blacks were at least partly civilized and Christianized by being brought from barbarous Africa. Furthermore, they were incapable of taking care of themselves and so slave owners were helping the blacks by assuming the responsibility.

Books and articles defending and attacking slavery appeared in large numbers. Two of the most significant, one for and one against the system, were written by southern authors. George Fitzhugh (1806-81) of Virginia compared the northern wage system of industrialism unfavorably with slavery in *Cannibals All!* (1857). Factory workers, he argued, were "slaves without masters," and had no guarantee of care in illness or in old age as did the slaves. As capital accumulated in fewer hands, Fitzhugh saw slavery eventually becoming the basis of the social system everywhere because only in that way could capital and labor live harmoniously.

At the other extreme was Hinton Rowan Helper (1829-1909), son of a poor farmer in North Carolina, who, in *The Impending Crisis of the South* (1857), was both antislavery and anti-Negro. He argued that no matter how well off a few plantation owners might be, the nonslaveholding white farmers suffered from the competition and from the way in which the slave system retarded the development of the whole section compared with the North. Helper's book enraged the South, but three years later the Republican party distributed 100,000 copies of a condensed version of it to aid in the election of Abraham Lincoln. After the war, Helper wrote three more books, all of which were vicious attacks on the blacks as an inferior race and one of which called for the extinction of the Negro race.

The 1850 census found 434,495 free blacks in the country. Ten years later the number had increased by about 50,000 to 488,070. Most lived in the border states, the upper South and the

Middle Atlantic states, with Maryland having the largest number, followed by North Carolina, Pennsylvania and New York. Many of the free blacks lived in cities: 12,500 in Philadelphia in 1860, for example, and 10,600 in New York. Although they were somewhat better off in the free states than in the South, they often found their lives little better than that of their fellows who were slaves. Educational facilities were few and inadequate, while jobs as skilled workers were hard to find. Many free states had laws that restricted the rights and movements of the blacks almost as much as did southern laws, while public attitudes did not differ greatly from those of southern whites. Hardly anywhere could a free black vote, and some states (Indiana in 1851 and Oregon in 1857, for example) passed laws forbidding any more Negroes even to move into the state.

By 1852, when a new president was to be elected, the Compromise was the central issue of politics. The Democrats, in their platform, declared the Compromise to be the final word on the slavery question and opposed any attempt to revive agitation about it in Congress. The Whigs also approved the Compromise, but not quite so firmly. Making it a three-cornered race, the Free Soil party condemned the Compromise and took an antislavery stand. At the Democratic convention, warring factions deadlocked the balloting for the presidential nomination for forty-nine ballots before choosing a "dark horse," Franklin Pierce (1804-69) of New Hampshire. Pierce, a strong supporter of the Mexican War, had served in it and rose to be brigadier general of volunteers. After that he had had an undistinguished career in politics, so colorless that he made no enemies and was acceptable to all factions. He was a strong defender of the Compromise and as time went on his sympathy for the southern point of view cost him the support of many northern Democrats. A handsome man, well-meaning but of mediocre ability, Pierce was the youngest man elected to the highest office up to that time.

The Whigs also went through a long process before choosing, on the fifty-third ballot, General Winfield Scott (1786-1866). Scott stood entirely on his military record, which was a distinguished one. His career began in the War of 1812, where he was one of the few successful American officers. In the Mexican War he was the top American commander and carried out a brilliant campaign that ended with the capture of Mexico City. The Free Soilers nominated John P. Hale (1806-73), a New Hampshire politician who had been expelled from the Democratic party because he refused to vote for the annexation of Texas. In 1852 he was in the Senate as an independent. Pierce won the election with 1,601,000 popular votes and 254 electoral college votes to 1,386,000 and 42 for Scott. Hale received only 155,000 votes.

One achievement during Pierce's term was the opening up of Japan to western trade, although the naval expedition that accomplished this was organized during Fillmore's administration. This expedition was under the command of Commodore Matthew Calbraith Perry (1794-1858), who was the brother of the hero of the Battle of Lake Erie in the War of 1812, Oliver Hazard Perry, and who had been a midshipman at the age of fifteen. He had held major naval commands for a number of years. Perry's squadron of four vessels arrived in Tokyo Bay on July 8, 1853. The Japanese officials, whose country had been almost entirely closed to foreigners since 1638, would have nothing to do with the Americans at first. They finally accepted a letter from President Fillmore and Perry's ships sailed away to give the Japanese time to think over the matter.

Perry returned to Tokyo in February 1854, with a stronger squadron. By presenting the Japanese with impressive evidence of the prowess of the western world, such as a small-scale steam locomotive, farming implements and a barrel of whiskey, Perry convinced them they should conclude a treaty with the United States. This treaty allowed the Americans to establish a consulate and to supply and repair their ships in certain ports. To follow up this first step in opening Japan to the rest of the world, Townsend Harris (1804-78) was appointed consul general to Japan in 1855. Harris, a New York merchant who was instrumental in establishing the College of the City of New York, soon exercised considerable influence with the Japanese government, gave good advice to a nation just coming out of isolation, and established the tradition of United States-Japanese friendship that was not broken until 1941. In 1857 and 1858 Harris negotiated agreements that allowed the United States additional privileges in Japan.

During Pierce's administration, the government also negotiated the Canadian Reciprocity Treaty of 1854, which settled disputes over fishing rights off the Atlantic coast and eliminated customs charges on certain commodities. Such events, however, were overshadowed by the legislative battle that arose in January 1854 over a plan to organize the territories of Kansas and Nebraska.

## 2 *From Controversy to Crisis*

ANY REMAINING hope that the Compromise of 1850 had settled the slavery question disappeared in 1854 when another bitter debate took place in Congress, this time over the proposed Kansas-Nebraska Act. Senator Douglas, who was head of the committee on territories and an active promoter of western settlement, introduced a bill to organize the territories of Kansas and Nebraska, the former west of Missouri, a slave state, and the latter west of Iowa, a free state. The bill provided for what Douglas termed "popular sovereignty," and which was sometimes called "squatter sovereignty," meaning that those who settled in the territory would have the right to decide for themselves whether or not slavery would be allowed.

Although southern delegates had not sponsored the legislation and although they contended that slavery could not constitutionally be kept out of the territories, they for the most part supported the bill. The South hoped that Kansas would become a slave state if enough slave holders moved in from Missouri and other slave areas. In the North, on the other hand, even those not strongly antislavery were infuriated. The Compromise of 1820 had presumably settled for all time the northern boundary of slavery west of the Mississippi when it admitted Missouri as a slave state but forbade slavery otherwise north of the southern boundary of Missouri. Even the southern boundary of Kansas was farther north than this. Douglas's bill, therefore, had the effect of repealing the earlier Compromise.

United southern congressmen and enough northern Democrats combined to pass the bill and on May 30, 1854, President Pierce signed it into law. Douglas had won, but at considerable cost to his political future in the North. He was accused of sponsoring the bill in order to get southern backing for a bid for the presidency in 1856. Whatever his motives, he was anxious to open the West to further settlement, to push back still further the Indian tribes, and to make a northern route preferable to a southern one for a proposed transcontinental railroad by increasing the population along the route.

The struggle for the control of Kansas, a struggle that gave the name "Bleeding Kansas" to the territory, began almost at once. Proslavery residents of Missouri moved in, although many of them were more interested in acquiring land than in slavery. Back east in New England, the Emigrant Aid Company was organized to promote the settlement of Kansas by antislavery men and women. It was active for several years, but in all sent only about 2,000 settlers to Kansas. When an election was held in March 1855, about 5,000 men from Missouri, called "Border Ruffians" by the free soilers, entered Kansas and voted a proslavery legislature into office. Later in the year, a Free State convention in Topeka drew up a constitution which prohibited slavery, although it also passed an ordinance forbidding blacks to enter the territory. By January 1856, Kansas had two governments.

Sporadic fighting broke out between the two sides and went on for months. In May, a proslavery force, including some "Border Ruffians," attacked the town of Lawrence, a free soil stronghold, burned several houses and other buildings and killed one man. Exaggerated accounts of the raid further aroused antislavery sentiment throughout the North. The free soilers, in turn, were responsible for the so-called Pottawatomie

Massacre later in May. The leader of this foray was John Brown (1800-59), who was born in Connecticut, had fathered a large family and had failed in a succession of occupations and business ventures. A fanatical abolitionist, he went to Kansas with five of his sons in 1855. With six other men, including four sons, Brown pounced on five proslavery settlers and brutally murdered them. Proslavery men, in turn, attacked the settlement of Osawatomie, defended by Brown and others.

The violence in Kansas was reflected in Congress in May 1856 after Senator Charles Sumner of Massachusetts delivered a strong antislavery speech which came to be called "The Crime Against Kansas." In it he unnecessarily insulted Senator Andrew P. Butler of South Carolina, who was not present. Two days later, Butler's nephew, Representative Preston S. Brooks, attacked Sumner as he sat at his desk in the Senate, beating him so badly with a cane that Sumner did not fully recover for three years.

An election for a legislature, held in Kansas in the fall of 1856, resulted in a clear victory for the Free State party after fraudulent proslavery votes were thrown out. Nevertheless, the proslavery group, about two weeks later, held a constitutional convention that drew up the Lecompton Constitution, so-called because that town was the headquarters of the slavery interests. Free soilers refused to vote in an election called to ratify the constitution and so the slavery forces won. The free soilers' legislature then called its own election on the Lecompton Constitution. Held in January 1858, this referendum, boycotted by the slavery forces, resulted in an overwhelming defeat for the constitution. In spite of this, Pierce's successor, President James Buchanan, submitted the constitution to Congress and recommended the admission of Kansas as a slave state. Senator Douglas condemned the move as contrary to popular sovereignty, and broke with Buchanan. This split the Democratic party, and Buchanan was denounced by many northern Democrats. Congress rejected the president's recommendation and Kansas remained a territory until January 1861, when, after many southern members of Congress from seceding states had resigned their seats, it was admitted to the Union as a free state.

Besides the Kansas-Nebraska Act, another event of 1854, involving three American diplomats, added to the bad feelings between North and South. For some years southerners and their Democratic allies in the North had schemed to acquire the island of Cuba and so expand slave territory. The Pierce administration instructed Pierre Soulé (1801-70) of Louisiana, then minister to Spain, to make an offer to buy the island. Soulé's intrigues and threats angered the Spanish government and the offer was refused. The administration in Washington then ordered Soulé, together with John Y. Mason (1799-1859) of Virginia, minister to France, and James Buchanan of Pennsylvania, then minister to Great Britain, to meet in Ostend, Belgium, to draw up a report and recommendation regarding Cuba. The document, which became known as the Ostend Manifesto, was supposed to be kept secret, but its contents leaked out. It stated that if Spain refused to sell Cuba, the United States would be justified in seizing the island by force to protect the institution of slavery. The clamor in the North and abroad was so great that the Pierce administration had to disavow its support of the report. Antislavery forces saw it as proof that the Democrats had surrendered to the South, while southern Democrats looked with favor on Buchanan as a possible presidential candidate.

The increasingly emotional controversy over such matters as the Fugitive Slave Law, Kansas and the Ostend Manifesto resulted in the start of a realignment of political parties and power. Many northern and southern members of both the Democratic party and the Whig party were at odds over slavery and so open to a change of allegiance. First to benefit from this situation was the American party, more popularly known as the Know-Nothings. The party grew out of the Order of the Star

Spangled Banner, which was founded in 1849 to fight what some Americans saw as the menace of Catholicism and foreign influence through immigrants. When asked what the policy of the order was, members' reply "I know nothing" resulted in the name. The first national convention of the American party was held in late spring 1854. Besides attracting nativists who feared all kinds of foreign plots, the party stood strongly for preserving the Union. It attracted voters in this way and benefited from disenchanted antislavery Democrats in the North and some Whigs in the South. For a new party, the Know-Nothings showed remarkable strength in the 1854 elections. They swept state offices in Massachusetts and almost won New York. They gained control of Baltimore and won many offices in New Orleans. Nationally, the party elected about seventy-five congressmen. This gave it the balance of power in Congress from 1855 to 1857, but it was never able to enact any of the laws its members sought to restrict immigration and naturalization, and its strength waned.

The other party that owed its origin to the slavery controversy became one of the two major parties. Several meetings of groups opposed to slavery and disgruntled with both the Democrats and the Whigs were held in 1854. Perhaps the first such gathering was in Ripon, Wisconsin, in February, but the meeting that first proposed "Republican" as the name of the new party was held in Jackson, Michigan, in July. The Republicans became a general rallying point for abolitionists, members of the Free Soil Party, antislavery Whigs and some antislavery Democrats. The Republicans gained further strength after 1856, when the American party collapsed. In the 1854 elections, the new party carried Wisconsin and Michigan and helped elect other candidates elsewhere.

Two years later, "Bleeding Kansas" was the chief issue of the presidential election. The honor of being the first Republican candidate for the office went to John C. Fremont (1813-90), explorer, soldier and politician. Born in Georgia, Fremont had led expeditions in various parts of the Far West since 1841, had helped secure California for the United States in 1846 and had been one of that state's first senators. Known as "The Pathfinder," and now a national hero, Fremont was nevertheless distrusted by some as a braggart, suspected of exaggerating his own deeds. The Democratic candidate was James Buchanan (1791-1868) of Pennsylvania, who had served in Congress, been secretary of state and held diplomatic posts abroad. Six feet tall, old-fashioned in dress and exceedingly dignified in behavior, Buchanan had sought the presidency for some years. The American party selected former president Millard Fillmore (1800-74) of New York, who as vice-president had presided over the Senate debate on the Compromise of 1850. The Whig party, what was left of it, also endorsed him. Fillmore began his political career in New York in the Anti-Masonic party, but by 1840 was a leader of the Whigs there.

In the campaign, Buchanan, who thought that slavery was morally wrong but that the Constitution protected it, was clearly the candidate of the South and the proslavery interests. Fillmore tried to assume a middle position but the steps he had taken when president to enforce the Fugitive Slave Law made him unpopular with northern Whigs. The Democrats called Fremont's party "Black Republicans," and the Republicans in turn blamed the Democrats for the bloodshed in Kansas. The new alignment brought the North and the West together as never before. In the election, Buchanan received 1,928,000 popular votes and 174 tallies in the electoral college; Fremont, 1,391,000 and 114. Fillmore had 847,000 votes and carried only Maryland with eight electoral votes. Nevertheless, the combined popular vote for Fremont and Fillmore was more than Buchanan received.

Buchanan's administration was a period of controversy and rancor and his actions did much to alienate further the voters of the North and West. Besides trying to get the Lecompton Constitution approved for Kansas, he made another attempt, through personal agents, to buy Cuba but was rebuffed by Congress, which refused to appropriate any money. His administration killed in Congress a homestead bill to make public land available to all, and he vetoed another intended to encourage the establishment of state agricultural colleges.

In the spring of 1857 Buchanan named a non-Mormon to replace Brigham Young, head of the Mormon church, as governor of Utah Territory. When Young refused to leave office, Federal troops were sent. Young retaliated by declaring martial law and calling out his militia. Over the winter the Mormons carried out some raids on army camps, but in the spring of 1858 Buchanan sent personal representatives who worked out a truce, and in June the new governor was installed. At the time, friction between Mormons and non-Mormons was acute. In September 1857, the Mountain Meadow Massacre took place in a small valley in southwestern Utah. An emigrant party of about 140 persons was attacked by a band of Indians and a few whites, the latter led by John D. Lee (1812-77), a fanatical Mormon. The Mormons encouraged the emigrants to lay down their arms and assured them of protection in their retreat. They were, however, set upon and all were killed except the children. Years later, in 1875, Lee was arrested, and in 1877 he was sentenced to be executed on the spot of the massacre.

The most divisive event of Buchanan's administration was the Dred Scott Decision, rendered by the Supreme Court on March 6, 1857, only two days after his inauguration. Dred Scott was a black slave whose owner took him from the slave state of Missouri to the free state of Illinois in 1834, and then to Wisconsin Territory, where slavery was prohibited by the Missouri Compromise. Later Scott returned to Missouri and in 1846, after his master's death, sued for his liberty on the grounds that his stay in a free state and a free territory ended his slavery. The case eventually reached the Supreme Court, the chief justice of which was Roger B. Taney (1777-1864). Taney, who had held the position since 1836, came from a wealthy slave-owning family of Maryland and had served in President Andrew Jackson's Cabinet. The court decided Scott could not sue because Negro slaves, and even free descendants of them, were not citizens. Going beyond the points at issue in this particular case, the court also said that Congress had no power to prohibit slavery in the territories and therefore the Missouri Compromise, already repealed by the Kansas-Nebraska Act, was unconstitutional. The ruling, a blow to popular sovereignty, was denounced in the North, although Senator Douglas declared the court was within its rights and should be obeyed.

One result of this decision, and a portent of the way opinion was moving, appeared in the voting in the mid-term elections of 1858. The Republicans made wide gains in the North and West, where the Democrats lost eighteen seats in the House, while a dozen of the Democrats who did win were anti-Buchanan. The administration lost control of the House as a result.

The 1858 election campaign was also marked by one of the finest debates on political issues the nation has ever heard. The debate brought together Senator Douglas, already a national figure, and Abraham Lincoln (1809-65), unknown outside the state of Illinois where the two were fighting for a seat in the Senate. Within the state, Lincoln was well known, had held influential positions in the state government, had been an active Whig before joining the Republican party and was a successful practicing lawyer. Lincoln, as the underdog, challenged Douglas, who agreed, and seven debates were held. Before they began their debates, Lincoln, in accepting the Republican nomination, quoted from the Bible: "A house divided against itself cannot stand." Then he added: "I believe this government cannot endure permanently half slave and half free." In one of the debates, he stated the Republican position on slavery: "We think it a moral, a social and a political wrong." Lincoln, however, denied the social equality of the black and white races.

The most significant encounter between the two men took place in Freeport and resulted in a statement by Douglas that became known as the Freeport Doctrine. Lincoln cleverly tried to pin down his opponent on the meaning of the Dred Scott Decision by asking him if the people of a territory could now in any lawful way exclude slavery before a state constitution was adopted. Douglas evaded a flat yes or no, but said slavery could be excluded "for the reason that slavery cannot exist a day . . . unless it is supported by local police regulation." In other words, if a territory did not provide for the protection of slave property, it would not be practical for an owner to bring slaves into the territory. This answer hurt Douglas badly with southern Democrats. During the campaign, Lincoln traveled 4,300 miles by train, carriage and riverboat, making sixty-three major speeches. Douglas traveled even further, 5,200 miles, and gave fifty-nine speeches lasting from two to three hours each, as well as numerous shorter talks. Lincoln and the Republicans won more popular votes, but the Democrats won enough seats in the legislature to return Douglas to the Senate. Lincoln, however, achieved national recognition and was now a power in the new Republican party.

The bitterness of political battles was, however, nothing compared with the fury that followed the act of violence perpetrated by John Brown, now more fanatical than ever, on October 16, 1859. Brown had a wild scheme for forming an abolitionist state in the Appalachian Mountains and was encouraged and financed by New England and New York abolitionists. These people included some leading intellectuals, although they apparently did not know exactly what Brown planned. With eighteen men, including five blacks, Brown captured the Federal armory at Harpers Ferry, Virginia, killed the mayor and took some citizens as hostages. Brown expected the slaves in the area to rally to him but none did. The state militia was called out and the Buchanan administration sent a force of marines under the command of Colonel Robert E. Lee of the army.

After a two-day siege, Brown surrendered. Two of his sons were dead, he was wounded and only four others were alive. Brown was tried for murder, treason and criminal conspiracy. Found guilty, he was hanged on December 2, going to his death with dignity and saying he was content "to die for God's eternal truth." John Brown's raid spread fear and anger throughout the South, where it was blamed on the abolitionists and the "Black Republicans." While responsible newspapers and public officials in the North repudiated the act, extreme abolitionists hailed Brown as a hero and a martyr. Even Ralph Waldo Emerson called him "that new saint."

The many harsh words and the acts of violence of the 1850's set the theme for the presidential election of 1860, the most divisive in the nation's history.

# 3 From Crisis to Secession

SLAVERY WAS the central issue of the 1860 presidential election, and many voters were worried that if the issue were not settled to the satisfaction of the proslavery forces, the Union would be broken up. That this was a real threat became clear as soon as the Democrats assembled in Charleston, South Carolina, in April. The southern delegates insisted on a platform that called for the protection of slavery in the territories. The northern delegates, led by Douglas, would not accept this, knowing that if they did they would lose the entire North.

Many southern delegates at this point walked out of the convention, which adjourned after deciding to meet again in Baltimore, Maryland, in June. Here more southerners defected, and the remaining Democrats then nominated Douglas. The southern Democrats assembled in Baltimore later in June, accepted an extreme proslavery platform and chose John C. Breckinridge (1821-75) as their candidate. Breckinridge, a lawyer from Kentucky, had served in the House, and at the time of his nomination was vice-president. Although a strong supporter of slavery and states' rights, he had presided impartially over the Senate in the recent troubled years. He believed in the right of a state to secede from the Union, but at this time he was opposed to such action. Later, even though his home state did not secede, he went with the Confederacy and served capably as a brigadier general.

A new party, called the Constitutional Union party, was organized, chiefly from former Whigs and some remnants of the American party. Its strength lay mostly in the border states and it had some appeal to southerners who were against secession. Delegates from twenty states nominated John Bell (1797-1869) for president. Bell was a lawyer, born in Tennessee, who had spent a good deal of his career in public office, having been senator from 1847 to 1859. He spoke for those southerners who supported slavery, but put the Union ahead of it. His party's platform said nothing about the burning issue, however, and merely declared it would uphold "the Constitution of the country, the Union of the States and the enforcement of the laws."

The Republican party, a sectional party of the North and West, was united in its position on slavery and was growing in strength. It met in Chicago in May in "the Wigwam," an enormous wooden structure that had been erected for the occasion and could hold 10,000 people. At first the leading candidate for its presidential nomination was William H. Seward of New York, who had been a national figure for a decade and was strongly antislavery. He angered the South when, in opposing the Compromise of 1850 in the Senate, he declared there was "a higher law than the Constitution." In a speech in 1858, he asserted that the nation was heading for "an irrepressible conflict" unless it became all slave or all free. The other main contender for the nomination was Abraham Lincoln, who was less well known and had held office in the national government only for a two-year term in the House. He was, however, a fresh personality who had made no political enemies within the party. On the third ballot, the Republicans chose Lincoln.

The Republican's second candidate for the highest office

was born in a log cabin in Kentucky of a very poor family. When he was seven, his family moved to Indiana, and later to Illinois. Lincoln grew into a gangling six feet four inches of height by the time he was seventeen and always remained rather awkward appearing, with a leathery complexion and coarse black hair. As a young man he farmed, made two trips to New Orleans on flat-bottom cargo boats and became a hard-to-beat wrestler. At the same time, with less than a year of formal schooling, he sought to educate himself. Lincoln was attracted to politics early, losing his first race in 1832, but winning a seat in the state legislature two years later as a Whig. Meanwhile, he was studying law on his own, and in 1836 was admitted to the bar. He moved from New Salem to Springfield the next year and this became his permanent home where he developed an active law practice. Friendly, compassionate and developing into a good speaker, Lincoln became widely known and respected in Illinois. He was influential in the state government, where he showed great talent for political dealing and for working out compromises. In 1841 Lincoln married Mary Todd (1818-82), from Kentucky. They were unalike in almost every way: she was short and plump and cared a great deal about dress and social position. Mary Todd Lincoln was also extravagant and at times mentally unbalanced, especially after the death of three of her four sons and the assassination of her husband. Their married life, though, seems to have been reasonably happy in spite of their different natures.

Lincoln's nomination was due in part to a speech he gave at the Cooper Union in New York City in February 1860. In carefully reasoned terms, he set forth his own and the Republican party's stand on slavery. He said that slavery should be contained but not attacked. He hoped that emancipation would come gradually and that it would be accompanied by settling the freed blacks in Latin America or Africa. It was a conciliatory speech but he refused to concede to the South any terms under which slavery could expand. At the end he brought his audience cheering to its feet when he said: "Let us have faith that right makes might, and in that faith let us, to the end, dare to do our duty as we understand it."

Four New York papers reprinted the speech in full, and it was widely reported around the nation. A few months later the lanky Illinois lawyer, whose clothes never seemed to fit quite right and whose legs were too long for the rest of his body, was the political leader of the antislavery forces of the nation. Lincoln ran on a platform that was not only antislavery, but also appealed to business and industry with its promise of internal improvements, a transcontinental railroad and a protective tariff. The platform promised western farmers easier access to public land ("vote yourself a farm").

In keeping with custom, Lincoln did not make campaign speeches and when queried as to his stand on the issues, especially slavery, he referred everyone to what he had already said. Douglas broke with tradition and was the first presidential candidate to move around the country making speeches in his own behalf. He was not in good health, but from July to November he traveled through the North and the South. The campaign was enlivened by many political rallies, with bands and speeches. Young Republicans formed groups they called the "Wide Awakes" and paraded with torches hoisted on fence rails in honor of Abe Lincoln, "the rail splitter," who as a youth had shown prowess with an ax.

There were now thirty-three states with electoral votes, Minnesota (1858) and Oregon (1859), both free states, having been admitted since the 1856 election. With eighteen free and fifteen slave states and the Democratic party split, a Republican victory was almost inevitable. Lincoln received 1,866,000 votes and 180 in the electoral college, carrying all eighteen free states, except that in New Jersey he shared the votes with Douglas. Breckinridge carried eleven of the slave states with seventy-two electoral tallies, but received only 845,000 popular votes. Bell, with 589,000 popular votes, won three slave states—Virginia, Kentucky and Tennessee—and thirty-nine electoral votes. Douglas was easily second in number of popular votes with 1,475,000, but he earned only twelve electoral votes, carrying the slave state of Missouri and receiving three of New Jersey's seven votes. Lincoln was in one sense a minority president, but even if his opponents' votes had been combined, he would have lost only eleven electoral votes and would still have had a majority in the electoral college.

Lincoln was president-elect but it would be about four months before he took office. Buchanan, meanwhile, had to deal with the aftermath of the election. Southern extremists made it clear they would not accept a Republican president, but many voices, both North and South, spoke for compromise. Among numerous such proposals, the Crittenden compromise attracted the most attention. This was put forward in Congress by John J. Crittenden (1787-1863) of Kentucky, who had served in the Senate and the cabinet for many years. His last-minute effort at compromise proposed constitutional amendments that would restore the old Missouri Compromise line and extend it to the California boundary. Any territory south of it would be slave, and Congress would be forbidden ever to interfere with slavery in any state where it existed. While the Republican party was willing to leave slavery alone and was not abolitionist, it would not accept anything that made it possible for slavery to expand one step. Lincoln made this clear. The Crittenden compromise failed in Congress, as did other proposals.

At the call of Virginia, a convention of the states was held in Washington in February 1861, and was presided over by former president John Tyler. Only twenty states sent delegates and their proposals, much like Crittenden's in effect, were unsuccessful also. The well-meaning but timid Buchanan, in the meantime, had been seeking a way out and had supported both these compromises. In his message to Congress in December 1860, he pleaded with the South not to secede and argued strongly that Lincoln's election was not a just cause for breaking up the Union. He also insisted that a state had no right to secede, but on the other hand he declared the president had no legal power to prevent it.

While attempts at compromise went on in Washington, secession was becoming a fact in the South. South Carolina, the state that had always been the most passionate defender of states' rights, seceded on December 20. By the beginning of February 1861, South Carolina was joined by six more states, in order: Mississippi, Florida, Alabama, Georgia, Louisiana and Texas. Delegates from all of these states except Texas (whose representatives arrived later) met in Montgomery, Alabama, on February 4 to organize the Confederate States of America. They drew up a constitution based on that of the United States, even using some of the same language. This new constitution, however, contained clauses to protect states' rights and, unlike the other constitution, it forthrightly used the word slave in sections giving legal protection to slavery as an institution. In some respects, as to the machinery of government, the southern document was an improvement over the older one.

In Washington, preparations went on to inaugurate a new president of a country whose future seemed dim. On March 4, a clear, windy day, with troops lining the streets and riflemen stationed on rooftops, Lincoln took the oath of office and delivered his inaugural speech. Although he seemed ill at ease at first, Lincoln spoke in a determined voice and attempted to show the South it had nothing to fear from his administration

I have no purpose directly or indirectly to interfere with the institution of slavery in the states where it exists. . . . In your hands, my dissatisfied fellow countrymen and not in mine, is the momentous issue of civil war. The government will not assail you. . . . You have no oath registered in heaven to destroy the government, while I shall have the most solemn one to "preserve, protect, and defend" it. . . .

President Lincoln also had to organize his cabinet and his administration to deal not only with the secession crisis but with all the ordinary details of government. He was under great pressure from hundreds, if not thousands, of Republican office seekers, anxious for political plums. He remarked wryly: "I am like a man so busy in letting rooms in one end of his house, that he can't stop to put out the fire that is burning in the other." Lincoln's cabinet, some members of which were to play leading parts in the war years ahead, included: William H. Seward (1801-72), secretary of state; Salmon P. Chase (1808-73), secretary of the treasury; Gideon Welles (1802-78), secretary of the navy; and Simon Cameron (1799-1889), secretary of war, who was replaced in less than a year by Edwin M. Stanton (1814-69).

Seward, who had been a senator since 1849, was generally acknowledged to be the leading Republican until Lincoln was nominated. Many people, including Seward, thought he would be the power behind the throne, the real head of the administration rather than the unknown and seemingly ineffectual Lincoln. In a remarkable memorandum dated April 1, Seward proposed to Lincoln that the United States pick a quarrel with Spain and France, and possibly other European nations, to bring on a war which would reunite North and South. He also hinted that he would be happy to manage the project. Lincoln cooly ignored Seward's scheme, and as time went on the two men became friendly and admirers of each other's abilities. Seward proved to be an adept diplomat in dealing with European nations during the war.

Chase, who had been born in New Hampshire, made his legal and political career in Ohio. An early leader among anti-slavery forces, he defended so many runaway slaves that he was known as the "attorney general for fugitive slaves." A senator since 1849, he fought the Compromise of 1850 and the Kansas-Nebraska Act. Although without experience in government finance, especially the extraordinary problems of financing a war, Chase was an able secretary of the treasury. Tremendously ambitious, he sought a presidential nomination each four years from 1860 to 1872. Chase resigned from the cabinet in 1864, and in December of that year Lincoln appointed him chief justice of the Supreme Court.

Welles quit the Democratic party over slavery and helped found the Republican party. Although without prior experience with regard to naval matters, he proved an able administrator, built up a powerful navy and supported the construction of ironclad warships. Cameron was, in effect, forced on Lincoln as a result of a political deal made at the nominating convention. He had made a fortune in various business ventures in Pennsylvania, where he also became a power in the Democratic party before switching to the Republicans. Within a short time, indications of corruption and favors in letting army contracts were so flagrant that Lincoln eased Cameron out of the cabinet and named him minister to Russia. His successor, Stanton, was a Democrat but strongly in favor of the preservation of the Union. Although rather ill-mannered and often opposing Lincoln's policies, he was nevertheless a good administrator. He ended much of the corruption and organized transportation and supply procurement so that the mammoth Union war machine was efficiently provided with what it needed.

While Lincoln was organizing his administration, the Confederate convention finished its work in Montgomery by electing Jefferson Davis (1808-89) provisional president. A full-scale election in November confirmed him for a six-year term. Davis, who was born in Kentucky as Lincoln was, seemed at this time a much abler and more experienced man than the northern president. He was a West Point graduate and a Mississippi cotton planter, his family having moved to that state. When the Mexican War began, Davis rejoined the army and commanded a Mississippi regiment with bravery and distinction. He was appointed secretary of war in 1853 and used his position to push for the expansion of slave territory and a southern route for a railroad to the Pacific. At the time of secession, Davis was the leader of the southern bloc in the Senate. He was a bit above medium height, with a square chin and thin lips, distinguished and rather austere looking. He was always dignified but had none of the personal warmth of Lincoln. As the war went on, Davis quarreled with other leaders of the Confederacy and was accused of acting in too arbitrary and high-handed a manner.

Nor did the South turn up as many capable civilian leaders as the North. Among those who held high office were Alexander H. Stephens (1812-83), Stephen R. Mallory (1813-73) and Judah P. Benjamin (1811-84). Stephens, elected vice-president of the Confederate States, was a Georgian who in Congress had favored the Compromise of 1850 and who was against secession but accepted the decision of his state when it left the Union. He and Davis clashed frequently. Mallory resigned from the Senate when his state, Florida, seceded and became secretary of the navy, where he advocated the building of ironclad vessels. Benjamin was a successful lawyer in Louisiana who also became a sugar planter. He served in the Senate as a Whig and under the Confederacy held three Cabinet positions successively: attorney general, secretary of war and secretary of state. Toward the end of the war he urged using slaves in the army and giving those who served their freedom. This angered many planters. In the North, Benjamin was known as "the brains of the Confederacy."

With rival governments in opposition to each other, a major practical problem facing Lincoln was what to do about Fort Sumter at the entrance to the Charleston, South Carolina, harbor. By March 1861 all forts in the South, except this one, Fort Pickens in Pensacola Bay, Florida, and two smaller posts off the Florida coast, had been seized by the Confederates. President Buchanan had made no attempt to hold or win back any forts. His only action had been to send an unarmed merchant ship, with men and supplies, to Fort Sumter on January 5. Confederate shore batteries forced it to turn back. After much discussion within his cabinet, Lincoln decided to act, and on April 6 he informed South Carolina that an expedition with supplies only, no men or ammunition, was on the way. This led the Confederates to demand the surrender of Sumter, which was commanded by Major Robert Anderson (1805-71), a veteran of Indian fighting and of the Mexican War. Anderson, although he had only a small force and his food was nearly exhausted, refused. The Confederates then began a bombardment at 4:30 A.M., April 12. By the afternoon of the next day, Anderson was forced to surrender. Whether, as some believe, Lincoln ordered the expedition solely to maneuver the South into firing the first shot can never be known. In any event, the Civil War had begun.

The North was aroused at this firing on the flag. Lincoln, on April 15, declared an "insurrection" existed and called on the states to supply 75,000 men from the militia to suppress it. He issued two proclamations declaring a blockade of the southern coastline and called for recruits for the regular army beyond the number authorized by law. Lincoln also spent money without waiting for an appropriation from Congress and did not call Congress into session until July 4, at which time it approved the steps he had taken.

In the meantime, the Confederacy assumed its final form. Virginia seceded five days after Sumter was fired on, and in May, Arkansas, Tennessee and North Carolina followed in that order. In the four border slave states—Kentucky, Missouri, Maryland and Delaware—opinion was divided but all stayed in the Union, although Kentucky declared its neutrality. Enough sentiment for the Union and against slavery existed in western Virginia so that secession from the rest of the state was voted and recognized by the government in Washington. This area was admitted as the state of West Virginia in 1863 with a constitution that provided for the gradual abolition of slavery.

The eleven states of the Confederacy, containing about 9,000,000 people, of whom 3,500,000 were slaves, faced the rest of the Union, with nearly 22,000,000 people and two-thirds of the real property.

The question inevitably arose: How and why had war between the states come about? The question, in fact, is still debated. It was a war over slavery, but that was not the sole cause. It was also a war brought on by the vexing problem of race relations that would arise with emancipation. Was it primarily a war to save the Union? Certainly there was strong feeling in the North that the Union should not and must not be destroyed. Even though the idea of the Union was an abstraction, it had a strong emotional appeal. Was the war primarily an economic struggle? Certainly the North was becoming more and more dominant in this respect. The South could well feel its economic interests were suffering and that it was paying for northern prosperity. Was the war over states' rights? Not particularly, although many in the South felt strongly on this point, which was related to the belief that the North was trying to control the Federal government to the South's detriment. Finally, was the war inevitable? After a century of debate, no one can be certain.

1941848

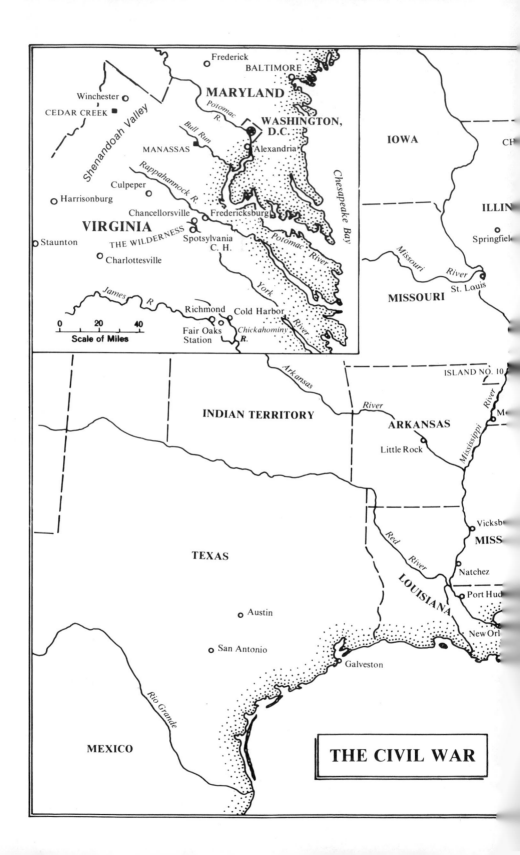

Frederick
BALTIMORE
**MARYLAND**
Winchester
CEDAR CREEK
*Shenandoah Valley*
Potomac R.
WASHINGTON, D.C.
Bull Run
MANASSAS
Alexandria
Rappahannock R.
Culpeper
Harrisonburg
Chancellorsville
Fredericksburg
**VIRGINIA**
THE WILDERNESS
Spotsylvania C. H.
Staunton
Charlottesville
Potomac River
Chesapeake Bay
James R.
Richmond
Cold Harbor
York River
Fair Oaks Station
Chickahominy R.

0    20    40
**Scale of Miles**

IOWA
ILLIN
Springfiel
Missouri River
St. Louis
**MISSOURI**
Arkansas
River
ISLAND NO. 10
INDIAN TERRITORY
**ARKANSAS**
Little Rock
Mississippi River
M
Vicksb
**MISS**
Red River
Natchez
**LOUISIANA**
Port Hud
**TEXAS**
Austin
San Antonio
New Orl
Galveston
Rio Grande
**MEXICO**

**THE CIVIL WAR**

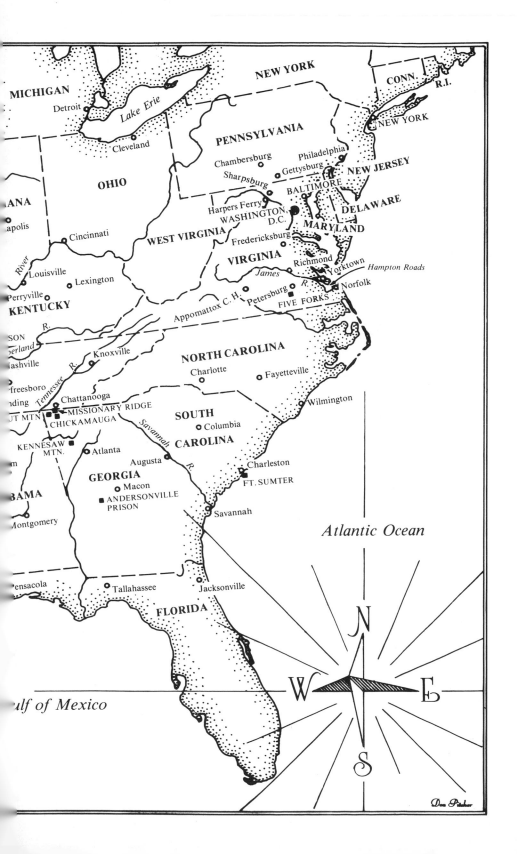

# 4 *From Bull Run to Murfreesboro*

THE UNITED States of America and the would-be Confederate States of America were an oddly matched pair of belligerents as they made preparations for war against each other. Besides the great discrepancy in population, the North also had an enormous advantage in basic economic strength. With six times as many manufacturing facilities and nearly ten times as many industrial workers, it could easily out-produce the South so far as firearms and other equipment were concerned. The North also possessed more than 70 percent of the railroad mileage and, just as important, it could replace rails, locomotives and cars as needed, whereas the South could not. With national banking centered in New York, the North was favored by a strong financial system, while the West, in alliance with the North, offered a prosperous and diversified agriculture well able to supply both soldiers and civilians with foodstuffs. Finally, the Federal government in Washington was a going concern, with diplomats abroad as well as a functioning bureaucracy at home.

The South, however, was not without advantages. It was on the defensive militarily and had only to hold off the North until the latter grew weary of fighting. The South held the offensive so far as morale was concerned: it had made the positive decision to secede and was determined to uphold the right to do so, while many people in the North were not sure blood should be shed to force the South back into the Union. By the nature of the southern way of life, there were more people who were used to firearms and outdoor living than there were in the North. Then, too, the South was confident that Europe—Britain and France in particular—would come to its aid because they needed the South's cotton.

In readily available military strength, neither side was prepared for war. The Federal government could call on the regular army, but that consisted of only 16,000 men, scattered around the nation. The navy possessed about forty vessels in commission, and these too were scattered. President Lincoln's call for 75,000 volunteers to serve for three months was met at once, and with enthusiasm. These troops, though, were poorly trained and had no experience in operating as parts of large units in the field. In early May 1861, Lincoln asked for 42,000 more volunteers and for 40,000 enlistments for three years in the regular army. Southern states began individual preparations for war as soon as each seceded, so that the Confederacy actually started arming earlier than the North. President Davis called for 100,000 volunteers for a year and had them all by the end of April.

The South's most important military advantage resulted from the way in which trained army officers chose sides when the showdown came. A career as an army officer had long had more appeal to southerners than to northerners, so that in 1861 most of the trained, experienced West Point graduates were from the South. Almost all chose to go with their states, and so resigned their commissions. As the war went on, many demonstrated a high order of military skill. The North, on the other hand, had to find its generals by trial and error and by bringing back from civilian life men who trained at West Point but who had left the army.

One native Virginian who did not support the South was General Winfield Scott, who, since 1841, had been the commanding general of the army. At seventy-five and in poor health, he was nevertheless the best general the United States had had since George Washington. A big man, six feet five inches tall and weighing 300 pounds, he was known as "Old Fuss and Feathers" because of his love of pomp. Someone once said of him that "when he walked he seemed almost a parade by himself." He advised Lincoln that at least 300,000 men and two or three years would be needed to defeat the South, but his advice, sound as it was, was rejected. His declining health forced Scott's resignation in November 1861.

Outstanding among the officers who followed the lead of their states was Robert E. Lee (1807-70) of Virginia. Son of the revolutionary war hero "Light Horse Harry" Lee, he had graduated second in his class at West Point and two years later married Mary Custis, great-granddaughter of Martha Washington. Lee served with distinction under General Scott in the Mexican War and later was superintendent of the United States Military Academy. At fifty-five, he was tall and handsome, with graying hair, a kind and courteous southern gentleman. Lee was opposed to both secession and slavery (he freed the few slaves he inherited), but he felt his first loyalty was to his native state. Although offered the field command of the Union army, Lee resigned with sorrow and went home to organize the forces of Virginia.

No major battle took place until July, and even then General Scott was calling for more time to train and equip the Union forces. The clamor from newspapers and politicians was such, however, that the government felt forced to order an attack. Accordingly, the Union army of 30,000 men advanced into Virginia and on July 21, 1861, fought the newly organized Confederate army at Bull Run, a small stream southwest of Washington. The fight also became known as the first battle of Manassas. The Union army was under the command of General Irvin McDowell (1818-85), a West Pointer who, like many officers on both sides, had served in the Mexican War. The Confederate commander was General Pierre G. T. Beauregard (1818-93), a West Point graduate from Louisiana who had taken part in the fighting at Mexico City. It was he who had ordered the first gun fired at Fort Sumter.

The North had a decided advantage until General Joseph E. Johnston (1807-91) brought 9,000 southern troops from the Shenandoah Valley. Johnston, a Virginian and a West Pointer, had been wounded five times in the Mexican War. McDowell's forces attacked first and turned one flank of the Confederate line. Victory seemed assured until, in mid-afternoon, more reinforcements arrived from the South and the green Union troops retreated. The retreat turned into a rout, all order was lost and equipment thrown away as the soldiers fled toward Washington. Caught up in the retreat were many civilians from Washington, men and women, government employees and politicians, who had come along as though on a picnic. Fortunately for the North, the Confederates, also inexperienced, were in no condition to give active pursuit. One reason for the southern victory was the stand of troops under the leadership of General Thomas J. Jackson (1824-63) at the crucial point in the battle. Jackson, another Virginian and West Point graduate who had fought in Mexico, rallied his troops and they stood their ground so firmly that he was thereafter known as "Stonewall" Jackson.

Union losses were nearly 3,000 men killed, wounded and missing, while the Confederate total was nearly 2,000. These figures shocked North and South alike, although they were nothing compared with the casualty figures to come in the next four terrible years. The South, of course, was jubilant; the North was sobered and competent observers realized the struggle was not going to be a short and easy one.

The defeated McDowell was replaced by General George B. McClellan (1826-85). Born in Pennsylvania, McClellan, like Lee, graduated second in his class at West Point and served in the

Mexican War. He resigned from the army in 1857 and was a railroad official until returning to the army in 1861. In November he replaced Scott as general-in-chief. McClellan was excellent at organizing and training an army and he always aroused great enthusiasm among his troops. On the other hand, he was so cautious and indecisive that critics doubted his will to fight. His unwillingness to attack was compounded by the man he placed in charge of his military intelligence, Allan Pinkerton (1819-84), head of the detective agency bearing his name which he had founded in 1850. Pinkerton invariably estimated Confederate troop strength at two or three times what it actually was and McClellan was only too happy to believe him because it provided an excuse for inaction. McClellan began rebuilding and enlarging the army, but he had no intention of fighting in 1861.

Military action shifted to the West in early 1862 when a campaign was begun to open the Mississippi River to Union ships, and thus split the Confederacy in two. Much of the early action took place along the Tennessee and Cumberland rivers, two large tributaries of the Mississippi. A combined force of army troops and navy gunboats forced the surrender of Fort Henry on the Tennessee on February 6. In command of the naval forces was Andrew H. Foote (1806-63) who, in 1843, as an officer on the *Cumberland*, made it the first ship in the navy on which liquor was banned. He was also largely responsible for ending the daily alcohol ration for the whole navy in 1862, and had been active in fighting the African slave trade. Before the end of the month, Foote was wounded in another battle, and later had to retire from active service.

In command of army forces at Fort Henry was Ulysses S. Grant (1822-85), a native of Ohio. Although considered a dull and bashful boy, Grant secured an appointment to West Point, from which he graduated in the middle of his class. In the Mexican War he was awarded a temporary captaincy for his gallantry at the battle of Chapultepec. He served in various army posts until 1854, when the combination of a colonel who didn't like him and his inability to handle liquor caused him to be threatened with court martial. Grant resigned and tried farming and several business ventures, none of which succeeded. When war broke out he was clerking in his family's leather store. His military background secured him an appointment as colonel of an Illinois volunteer regiment and by August 1861, he was a brigadier general. Grant seldom looked like a general. He was careless of dress and tended to slouch in an unmilitary manner.

Grant soon proved to possess some vital qualities many other Union generals lacked: determination and a willingness to carry the fight to the enemy wherever and whenever possible. The whole Union heard of him on February 16, 1862, when after a three-day siege by his forces, Fort Donelson on the Cumberland in Tennessee, commanding the river approach to Nashville, surrendered. Grant received 15,000 Confederate prisoners after demanding "immediate and unconditional surrender," a phrase that was cheered throughout the North. The fall of Fort Henry and Fort Donelson forced the Confederates to abandon Nashville, Tennessee, after which they sought to regroup at Corinth, Mississippi, a vital railroad junction.

While the Union forces were moving south along the Tennessee River, General Albert S. Johnston (1803-62), commanding the Confederate forces, hoped to strike Grant's army before it reached full strength. Johnston, another West Point alumnus, had joined the Texas army fighting for independence against Mexico in 1835 and had become its commander in 1837. He also served in the Mexican War. In charge of all the southern forces in the West, Johnston was considered one of the ablest generals on either side.

Grant halted his forces at Pittsburg Landing, on the Tennessee, and here Johnston attacked him. Generally known as the battle of Shiloh because it took place near a meetinghouse called

Shiloh Church, the fight was by far the bloodiest to date. Grant's troops had not prepared defenses and were not ready to fight because he expected to move on and take the initiative himself. Accordingly, the Confederate attack on April 6 was successful, and in confused fighting the Union troops were nearly pushed into the river. Holding on by their own determination and Grant's will, the Union army fought back the next day after reinforcements arrived. Johnston was killed in the first day's fighting and General Beauregard, who succeeded him, finally withdrew. The Federal troops suffered about 13,000 casualties and the South over 10,000. Grant was severely criticized for being caught unawares. Although the battle was a draw in that neither army was routed, the Confederates had failed to regain the initiative and from then on they were almost always on the defensive in the West.

On the second day of Shiloh, another Union force captured Island No. 10 in the Mississippi when troops under General John Pope (1822-92) invaded the island after Foote's gunboats had destroyed the Confederate batteries there. Pope, a Kentuckian, had his training at West Point and made a distinguished record in the Mexican War.

New Orleans, key to the mouth of the Mississippi River, fell to the Union navy on April 28 as a result of a bold attack led by Captain David Glasgow Farragut (1801-70). Farragut, a career navy officer, had a force of eight sloops-of-war and fifteen gunboats. After attacking the two forts guarding the river approach to the city, Farragut's ships slipped past them, defeated such vessels as the Confederates could put into action, and forced the South to abandon the important port and trading city. The Union troops that occupied the city on May 1 were commanded by General Benjamin F. Butler (1818-93), a Democratic politician from New England who was strongly against secession. Although he was energetic in raising some of the first troops sent to defend Washington, he was incompetent as a military leader. His rule of New Orleans was so high-handed that southerners called him "Beast" Butler, and President Davis declared him an outlaw, subject to execution if caught. President Lincoln removed him from New Orleans in December 1862.

Action in the East in 1862 began with a unique sea battle, the first engagement ever fought between ironclad vessels. When the Union forces abandoned the Norfolk navy yard at the start of the war, they burned and scuttled ships there, including the steam frigate *Merrimack*. The Confederates raised the ship but instead of rebuilding her upper decks they sheathed the hull in iron and renamed her the *Virginia*, although the name *Merrimack* has been retained in refering to the battle. On March 8 the new ironclad attacked wooden Union ships in Hampton Roads, sinking and grounding several. When the *Merrimack* returned the next day to finish off the grounded ships, she was met by the *Monitor*, which looked like "a cheesebox on a raft." The *Monitor* was designed by John Ericson (1803-89), Swedish-born inventor and engineer, who had earlier devised the screw propellor which revolutionized ship navigation. The main feature of the ironclad *Monitor* was a circular, armored revolving gun turret. The two ships battled for several hours, neither being able to do much damage to the other. The fight signaled the end of the era of wooden warships, although the Confederates had to destroy the *Merrimack* in May when they were forced out of Norfolk.

By February 1862, McClellan had been enlarging and training the Union army around Washington for eight months, and Lincoln was losing patience at his failure to take the field. The president and his cabinet wanted a direct march on Richmond, now the Confederate capital, but they finally let McClellan have his way. His plan called for transferring the army by sea to the peninsula formed by the York and James rivers, from where the force would advance westward on Richmond. Finally, in mid-March, McClellan began his move, although not before Lincoln had removed him from command of the entire army, leaving him with the Army of the Potomac only. This army, now 100,000 strong, was the most formidable force ever seen in America.

At Yorktown on the peninsula, the Confederates were vastly outnumbered, but McClellan refused to attack. Over-cautious as usual, he began preparations for a siege, only to find after a month that the Confederates had abandoned Yorktown. By the end of May, the Union army was spread out on both sides of the Chickahominy River, the smaller segment on the south bank being isolated from the rest because of flood conditions. Here, near Fair Oaks Station, the southern army under Joseph E. Johnston attacked on May 31, and the Union forces barely escaped a disastrous defeat. The Confederates suffered greater casualties, about 8,000 to 6,000 for the North, and General Johnston was seriously wounded. As a result, Robert E. Lee, who had been carrying out various advisory tasks for President Davis, took command of the Army of Northern Virginia on June 1. This was a fateful decision that led to some of the most glorious moments of the Confederate forces.

Lee determined to drive McClellan off the peninsula and began an offensive that resulted in the Seven Days' battle of June 26 to July 2. The Union forces withdrew to a position on the James River where they would have the protection of their gunboats. McClellan's troops successfully held off the Confederate attacks and Lee was forced to withdraw toward Richmond. The South suffered over 20,000 casualties, the North nearly 16,000. The Army of the Potomac was in no condition to fight any more and so ended a campaign at the start of which McClellan had promised to take Richmond in ten days. Not until the end of the war, nearly three years later, did the Union army again get so near the Confederate capital.

Johnston's and Lee's defense of Richmond had been aided materially by a diversion "Stonewall" Jackson created in the Shenandoah Valley, which pointed northeast like a dagger at the heart of the North and could be used to approach Washington from the west. Between late March and early June, Jackson managed to bedevil several Union commanders, with about three times as many troops as he had, to such an extent that an anxious Lincoln and Stanton sent 20,000 more soldiers there. These troops had been intended for use in the attack on Richmond.

After a year of war, the North was back where it had started and Lincoln, in July 1862, tried a new general as commander of the whole army: Henry W. Halleck (1815-72). A West Pointer, Halleck had written a book on fortifications which was used by both sides during the war. Before being called to Washington, he had been in overall command in the West and his indecisiveness there had prevented Grant and others from achieving as much as they might have. Even so, they made Halleck look like a victorious general, but he was more an organizer than a battlefield commander who pressed hard for victory.

Halleck put General Pope in command of all the eastern forces except McClellan's army, which was just starting back from the peninsula, and ordered Pope to march overland toward Richmond. Seeing a chance to strike this army before McClellan's troops could join it, Lee, with the aid of swift, baffling attacks by Jackson, routed Pope on August 30 in the second battle of Bull Run, causing 15,000 Union casualties, although southern losses were also heavy.

Lee now determined to invade Maryland and Pennsylvania. While he was preparing for this venture, McClellan took over Pope's beaten army as well as his own and combined them. Many voices were raised against giving this post to McClellan, but the army badly needed reorganizing after its demoralizing defeats and the soldiers still had faith in the general, even if many high officials in Washington did not. Lee marched into Maryland in early September and on the fifteenth Jackson captured Harpers Ferry with 11,000 Union troops and large quantities of supplies.

Two days later, McClellan's army of about 70,000 forced the Confederates, numbering about 40,000, to fight the battle of Antietam, near Sharpsburg, Maryland. For a while the Union attack gained, but McClellan did not take proper advantage of his opportunity. The battle ended more or less as a draw, but Lee had to withdraw to Virginia, no longer having the strength to attempt an invasion of the North. The total casualties on both sides were more than 23,000, almost evenly divided, and Antietam went down in history as the bloodiest single day of a bloody war.

McClellan dismayed the North by not pursuing Lee after Antietam, many people believing that the war might have been ended if the general had been more daring and energetic. Again, as throughout the war, Lincoln changed generals, this time naming Ambrose E. Burnside (1824-81), who had previously shown some competence. With a force of 113,000 compared with Lee's 75,000 Burnside attacked the Confederates at Fredericksburg, Virginia, where they held high ground on the south bank of the Rappahanock River. Burnside ordered several foolhardy assaults on Lee's strong position on December 13, resulting in a repulse that left 12,000 Union dead and wounded. Gloom and depression spread through the North. Burnside, who originated the style of long side whiskers known as burnsides or sideburns, was relieved of his command.

In the western theater of operations, a Confederate force under General Braxton Bragg (1817-76), who had been promoted for distinguished service in the Mexican War and who had led a corps at Shiloh, attempted in the fall to invade Kentucky with his Army of the Tennessee. A Union army under Don Carlos Buell (1818-98), who also had fought in the Mexican War and whose arrival with reinforcements saved the day at Shiloh, brought Bragg to battle at Perryville, Kentucky, on October 8. The result was not decisive but Bragg began a retreat to Tennessee the next day. Buell was so slow and inept in following Bragg that he was removed and his command given to William S. Rosecrans (1819-98), a former army officer who had rejoined as a volunteer in April 1861. His troops, now called the Army of the Cumberland, met Bragg's at Murfreesboro, Tennessee, on December 31. The Confederates almost routed the Union army the first day, but after a day's pause another attack by Bragg was repulsed and he was forced to retreat.

And so the year 1862 ended with Union gains in the West but stalemate in the East.

# 5 From Chancellorsville to Appomattox

AFTER THE battle at Fredericksburg in December 1862, Lee's army remained in the strong positions it held along the Rappahanock, while the Army of the Potomac reorganized once more, under another general. The new commander was Joseph Hooker (1814-79), nicknamed "Fighting Joe," who had been three times officially noticed for gallantry in the Mexican War and had served ably earlier in the war in subordinate capacities. With 130,000 men to Lee's fewer than 60,000, Hooker advanced his army and engaged Lee in the battle of Chancellorsville, west of Fredericksburg, beginning May 2, 1863. "Stonewall" Jackson took the Union left completely by surprise, while Lee drove back the rest of the northern army. Hooker retreated across the river on May 5, badly beaten. Casualties were heavy on both sides, but the Confederates lost the irreplaceable Jackson when his own men mortally wounded him by mistake as dusk fell.

Lee followed up this success in June by launching another invasion of the North, hoping a major victory on Union soil would break the will of the northern forces and the Federal government. The Army of Northern Virginia moved up the Shenandoah Valley and by June 23, 1863, was near Chambersburg, Pennsylvania. Hooker followed on Lee's flank but he suddenly resigned his command on June 27 as the result of a dispute with General Halleck over reinforcements. In his place,

Lincoln appointed George Gordon Meade (1815-72). Meade was a West Point graduate and had served in the Mexican War but most of his career had been spent as a civil engineer. Reentering the army in 1861, he showed his military skill at both Fredericksburg and Chancellorsville after being badly wounded in the Seven Days' battle.

Both generals picked sites on which they preferred to fight the other army, but neither was sure just where the enemy's main force was. Lee was handicapped in this respect because for once his "eyes" failed him. The eyes were the cavalry forces under the command of dashing James Ewell Brown (Jeb) Stuart (1833-64), a Virginian who had distinguished himself as early as the first battle of Bull Run. He made a complete circuit of McClellan's army in June 1862, supplying Lee with valuable intelligence in the peninsula campaign. Now, though, Stuart was off on one of his daring raids and for several days he sent no information to Lee. Parts of the two armies stumbled on each other on June 30 near Gettysburg, Pennsylvania. The next day, major forces fought there and the Confederates drove Meade's men back to a north-south line on Cemetery Ridge and Culp's Hill. Meade not only had a strong defensive position there, but also his force of more than 90,000 men outnumbered Lee's by about 15,000.

Lee, nevertheless, ordered an attack on July 2, the main thrust to be made by troops under General James Longstreet (1821-1904) on the Confederate right. Longstreet, a South Carolinian, a West Pointer and a veteran of the Mexican War, had served well in previous battles, but this time he delayed his attack until the Federal troops were reinforced. The attack failed. Lee insisted on another attack the next day at the strongest part of the Union line, to be led by General George E. Pickett (1825-75). Picket was a daring Virginian and West Point graduate who had distinguished himself in the Mexican War and in earlier fighting in the Civil War, and had been wounded in the Seven Days' battle. After an artillery bombardment, 15,000 men of the South charged Cemetery Ridge, but they were so chopped up by artillery and rifle fire that less than half a company ever reached the Union lines. These men were all killed or captured, and while Pickett himself survived in the midst of the carnage, his division was almost wiped out.

The battle of Gettysburg was over and Lee was defeated. His army suffered about 25,000 casualties, while Meade's had about 23,000 killed, wounded and missing. On the afternoon of July 4, Lee began to retreat. The Potomac was flooded and Lincoln urged Meade to pursue and finish off the Army of Northern Virginia before it could get across. Meade, hindered by rain and by the condition of his army, did not move and Lee escaped. The greatest battle of the war and the most important fought on American soil did not end the war, but it marked a turning point. The South was never again able to take the offensive.

While the southern cause was declining in the East, another fatal blow was struck on the Mississippi River. There Vicksburg, Mississippi, strongly defended, was the key to mastery of the river. Union forces had been trying to capture it for many months. The campaign began in earnest in late March when Grant, finding no way to get at the fortress directly, moved his army across the Mississippi north of Vicksburg. The troops marched south of the city, while gunboats and transports under the command of David D. Porter (1813-91) made a nighttime dash past the Vicksburg batteries. Porter had led part of the fleet under Admiral Farragut that took New Orleans, and next to Farragut was the leading naval commander of the war. The ships ferried Grant's troops back to the east bank, from where they marched on the city. General John C. Pemberton (1814-81), a northerner by birth who had chosen the Confederate side, was forced back inside the city. Grant tried two assaults which failed and then settled down for a siege. Bombarded for six weeks and near starvation, Pemberton's forces surrendered July 4, 1863, just as Lee retreated from Gettysburg. A few days later, Port Hudson, Louisiana, surrendered, leaving the Union in control of the full length of the river.

General Rosecran's army in Tennessee was trying to take Chattanooga, the key to communications between the East and the Mississippi. He maneuvered General Bragg out of the city on September 9, but the Confederates sent reinforcements in the form of General Longstreet and his corps. The two armies met at Chickamauga, near Chattanooga, on September 19 and 20, where the Confederate attack broke the Union line. The day was saved by General George H. Thomas (1816-70), a West Pointer from Virginia who chose to stay with the Union. Thomas's men, with bayonets, finally stopped the attack, earning Thomas the title of "Rock of Chickamauga," but the northern forces were forced to retire into the city where they were besieged by Bragg.

At this point, with Rosecrans obviously incompetent to carry on, Lincoln named Grant supreme commander of all the western forces, and the general himself headed for Chattanooga, arriving there October 23. His first step was to reopen the supply lines coming into Chattanooga. By November 23 he was ready to give battle to Bragg's forces which were entrenched on Lookout Mountain and Missionary Ridge. The Confederates were driven off Lookout Mountain in what was known as "the battle above the clouds." General Thomas's troops were then told to take the Confederate positions at the foot of the ridge on November 25, but they refused to stop there. In an incredible feat of climbing and fighting, they continued up the ridge and put Bragg's troops to rout. Bragg retreated into Georgia, and the Confederacy to the south and southeast lay open to a Union advance.

After three years of shuffling generals around, Lincoln had at last found one who had the will to win and the ability to pick like-minded subordinates. Grant was appointed commander of all the Union armies in March 1864, and Congress revived the rank of lieutenant general for him. Taking personal command of the Army of the Potomac, now numbering 118,000 men, Grant began a march directly on Richmond. He plunged into the Wilderness, a tangled woodland near Fredericksburg, where on May 5 and 6, 1864, a wild and disjointed battle took place. The fight was indecisive, but Grant marched on, trying to out-flank Lee and his smaller army of 60,000. Still nearer Richmond, at Spotsylvania Courthouse, the armies fought again for several days, and again indecisively. It was at this time that Grant sent back to Washington his message: "I propose to fight it out along this line if it takes all summer."

A few miles northeast of Richmond, at Cold Harbor, Grant's men charged a strong Confederate defense on June 3, with 7,000 Union soldiers falling in a few hours. By this time, a month of fighting had cost the North 60,000 casualties, com-pared with 25,000 to 30,000 suffered by Lee's army. Grant's army, however, could be reinforced regularly, whereas the South was running short of manpower and never recovered from this brutal series of battles.

Once more Grant shifted his army, this time to Petersburg, southeast of Richmond, where he hoped to cut the Confederate capital's communication and supply lines with the rest of the South. A four-day battle, however, failed to take Petersburg, and the Army of the Potomac began to dig in for months of trench warfare. An enormous mine was exploded under Lee's lines on July 30, but troops under General Burnside did not follow up the advantage the surprise gave them and the affair became another bloody loss for the North. Grant, however, was slowly but surely winning the war of attrition. He kept extending his lines to the west, forcing Lee to weaken his defenses, while his shrinking, hungry army began to lose its strength and its verve.

The fruitful Shenandoah Valley was again the scene of attack and counterattack in the summer of 1864. The two chief antagonists were Jubal A. Early (1816-94) and Philip H. Sheridan (1831-88). Early, a West Pointer and a Virginian, had voted against secession in his state, but had been a useful Confederate commander in most of the major engagements of the war in the East. Sheridan was from Ohio and had graduated from West Point after having been suspended a year for misconduct. He demonstrated military talent in the West, especially at Missionary Ridge, and Grant brought him East to command the cavalry of the Army of the Potomac.

Early moved north into Maryland in June, then southeast toward Washington, coming within five miles of the capital on July 11. Grant had to rush two divisions from Petersburg to defend the panicky capital. Determined to end the use of the Shenandoah Valley by the Confederates, Grant placed Sheridan in command of the Army of the Shenandoah and in two engagements in September, Sheridan soundly beat Early. He then proceeded to lay waste the valley, burning houses and barns, destroying crops and carrying off animals so that, as he said, a crow flying over it would have to carry its own rations. Early, however, was not quite finished. Catching Sheridan's troops at Cedar Creek on October 19, when the general was at Winchester, fifteen miles away, the Confederates routed the Union men. Riding desperately to the scene, Sheridan, whose fighting spirit was much admired by his soldiers, rallied them and counterattacked victoriously.

While Grant and Lee were fighting each other to a standstill, the war in the West was one of movement. Grant, in March 1864, made General William Tecumseh Sherman (1820-91) commander of the Union armies in the West. Sherman, an Ohioan who like so many on both sides had been at West Point and in the Mexican War, had shown his mettle at Shiloh, Vicksburg and Missionary Ridge. With 100,000 men Sherman left Chattanooga in early May with his objective the city of Atlanta, Georgia, 140 miles to the southeast. He was opposed by Confederate forces under General Joseph E. Johnston. Sherman kept outflanking

Johnston until he attacked him on June 27 at Kennesaw Mountain, twenty-five miles northeast of Atlanta. Sherman's men were repulsed with considerable losses. In mid-July, President Davis, who had been after Johnston to halt Sherman's advance, replaced him with General John B. Hood (1831-79), who before the war had served in California and Texas. Hood had been in the peninsula campaign, the second battle of Bull Run and others, including Chickamauga, where he lost a leg. Hood attacked Sherman three times, with inferior numbers, and finally had to retreat into the city itself, whereupon Sherman besieged it and cut the rail lines that led into it from several directions. Hood decided to abandon the city on September 1, and the next day Sherman's army marched in.

At the time Atlanta was being besieged, Admiral Farragut and the ships in his command struck another blow at the deep South and its ability to continue the war. Farragut had bottled up almost every port on the Gulf of Mexico, but supplies were still getting through the blockade to Mobile, Alabama. He determined to close Mobile Bay and on August 5, 1864, led his fleet in, past two forts and through a mine field (mines were called torpedoes at that time). Warned of the mines, he said: "Damn the torpedoes, full speed ahead," and routed the Confederate ships defending Mobile Bay and the city. Two years later, Congress made Farragut the first full admiral in the history of the American navy.

Sherman turned Atlanta into a strong point while he rested and refitted his army. On November 15 he was ready to leave and so ordered all buildings of military use burned. Carelessness resulted in a fire that spread beyond such buildings and burned down most of the city. The next day, Sherman's 60,000 men, in three broad columns, set out southeastward for Savannah. They lived well off the Georgia farm harvest, and destroyed what they could not use. It was Sherman's deliberate intention to devastate the land, both to demonstrate to the South the futility of further resistance and to deny supplies to the Confederate armies. As usual in war, the soldiers went beyond their orders in looting and pillaging. With no opposition, Sherman's army reached Savannah in twenty-four days and on December 21 captured the city. The Union troops had marched through the heart of the South to the sea, and on Christmas Eve Sherman telegraphed Lincoln, offering him the city as a Christmas present.

General Hood, not strong enough to directly oppose the Union march to the sea, tried to prevent it by moving north and west of Atlanta in an attempt to cut Sherman's supply lines and draw him in that direction. Sherman, however, needed no supplies and decided that General Thomas was able to deal with Hood. Hood got as far as Nashville, which had become a major Union stronghold, where he faced superior forces under Thomas. Thomas struck Hood's army on December 15 and 16, 1864, and almost destroyed it. It was the only time a Confederate army was completely routed. There was no longer any Confederate force of consequence in the western theater.

The last months of the war began with Sherman's next move. He left Savannah on January 16, 1865, and headed into South Carolina. Here, feeling they were in the center of the secession movement that had caused the war, the Union troops wrought even more destruction than in Georgia. Eighty city blocks of Columbia, the state capital, were burned to the ground on February 17—whether by Sherman's men deliberately or by accident, or by the retreating southerners, has never been settled. The next day, Charleston, the heart of secession, was taken. About a month later, Sherman fought in North Carolina the last force opposing him, the now small army of General Johnston, and pushed it back. Sherman said that "war is hell," and he was one of the first to accept that, in modern war, the defeat of opposing armies is not the whole of warfare. War is total, and includes breaking civilian morale and destroying the food and equipment needed to wage war.

As spring came, Grant was slowly grinding down Lee's ability to resist. Lee made his last effort on April 1, when he tried to break Grant's left flank. This move failed when, at Five Forks, near Petersburg, Sheridan's troops beat back those of Pickett. The next day, Lee abandoned Richmond, a great deal of which went up in flames the following day, and headed west, hoping to get his army to North Carolina to join up with the remnants of Johnston's army.

But Lee's now small army of 30,000 could not escape the more than 100,000 Union men in its path and on April 7 Lee asked Grant for surrender terms. When they met at Appomattox Court House on April 9, Lee was faultlessly dressed in his general's uniform, his bearing grave and dignified as always. Grant's uniform, by contrast, was rumpled and, except for the insignia on his shoulders, might have been that of one of his privates. The two generals quickly and calmly concluded their task. Lee's troops were to lay down their arms, but officers would be allowed to keep their sidearms and both officers and men could retain any horses or mules that belonged to them. In addition, Grant ordered the immediate distribution of 25,000 rations to the hungry Confederates. Jefferson Davis even at that point urged Johnston to keep on fighting but on April 18 he surrendered to Sherman in North Carolina. The fighting that no one had thought would last more than a few weeks had gone on for four tragic years.

While the war on land swept from Pennsylvania to the Gulf of Mexico and from the Mississippi River to the Atlantic Coast, a sea war of importance had also been waged. One part of it, the blockade of the coast of the Confederate states, quietly but effectively helped defeat the South. The other part, involving raids on northern merchant shipping by Confederate warships, was more spectacular and had international repercussions but little bearing on the result of the war.

When Lincoln declared a blockade of the 3,500 miles of

coastline of the Confederacy in April 1861, he created a problem in international law. His step, in a way, admitted the existence of a Confederate government which in every other context he denied. The European powers declared their neutrality, which also implied a certain recognition of the South and its rights as a belligerent. In any event, the Union had to make good the blockade declaration by actually shutting off southern ports. The navy, like that of other nations, was in the process of moving from the age of sail to the age of steam. Beginning with only forty-two vessels in service in March 1861, the Union navy expanded to 671 ships by December 1864. New ships were built and others purchased, including almost anything that would float—ferryboats and excursion boats, for example. Gradually the blockade became effective, for while incoming and outgoing traffic was never completely cut off, the South's seaborne commerce was, for practical purposes, shut down. All through the war, part of the blockade effort also consisted of capturing the forts and harbors of the South.

At sea the South attempted to retaliate in two ways. Early in the war, Davis encouraged privateering, but as the blockade took effect there was little incentive for this. More effective were the Confederate raiders, eighteen ships built in Europe, mostly in Great Britain. They roamed the seas sinking merchant ships, and they destroyed 257 in all. Most famous and successful of these ships was the *Alabama*, which in a two-year career in the Atlantic and the Pacific captured sixty-two merchant ships and sank one United States warship. It was commanded by Raphael Semmes (1809-77), who had served in the navy in the Mexican War. The *Alabama* was finally brought to bay off Cherbourg, France, on June 19, 1864, and sunk by the U.S.S. *Kearsarge*. Although the South's raiders had no practical effect on the war, they struck a blow at the American merchant marine from which it did not recover for half a century. Because of the danger and because of high insurance rates, the ownership or registration of about 700 American ships was transferred so they could sail under the flags of neutral nations.

The handling of prisoners taken in the Civil War posed special problems. If secession was constitutionally wrong, then all Confederate soldiers were rebels in armed revolt against their legitimate government. The North, however, chose to treat those captured in accordance with the rules of war. Thus in July 1862, arrangements were made to exchange prisoners man for man, while any surplus on one side would be released on parole not to take up arms again. There were charges of bad faith on both sides and the Confederates refused to treat captured black soldiers as prisoners of war. The exchange system broke down, and in the spring of 1864, Grant ordered that no more prisoners be exchanged. Charges were also made on both sides that prisoners were ill-treated, but on the whole it appears that they did not suffer much more than the soldiers in the two armies in a war in which sanitation facilities and medical care were extremely inadequate.

Andersonville prison in Georgia became particularly notorious. Opened in February 1864, it had 31,000 prisoners by July, in a sixteen-and-a-half-acre enclosure. Conditions were without doubt frightful. How many Union soldiers died there is in dispute, but there are 12,912 graves. After the war, Henry Wirz, the Confederate officer who had been in charge of Andersonville, was convicted and executed, but it is doubtful that he deliberately tried to create the horrible conditions that existed and grew beyond his control. In all, in the course of the war, the South captured 211,000 Federal troops while the Union armies took 462,000 prisoners.

The black population, both free and slave and North and South, presented some special problems in relation to war conditions. Union troops found most slaves eager to escape from their masters and seek protection with the army. What then was their status? After all, slavery was still legal in four states that remained in the Union. General Butler decided that fleeing slaves were contraband—that is, property belonging to and of use to the enemy and therefore subject to confiscation. The cabinet agreed on May 30, 1861, and while the problem of caring for these refugee slaves was not inconsiderable, they provided a labor force for the army.

Debate also took place within the Union army and government as to whether or not blacks should be allowed to enlist. It was not until August 25, 1862, that the War Department authorized recruiting Negro soldiers. By the end of the war nearly 180,000 had served, most of them free northern blacks. With very few exceptions, all their officers were white. Nearly 30,000 black soldiers were killed or died of wounds.

In the South, the Confederacy made use of its slaves behind the lines. Left unsupervised when owners went to war, many blacks took on more responsibilities on plantations, while others found they could shirk their usual tasks. The government used slaves to dig field fortifications, and in hospitals and factories, but most opinion was against allowing slaves to serve in the Confederate army. Lee urged in January 1865 that they be recruited, but it was not until March 13 that the government in Richmond authorized recruiting up to 300,000 slaves. By then it was too late, and none ever saw action.

In terms of casualties, the Civil War was the most devastating ever fought by the United States, especially considering the size of the population at the time. Enlistments were for varying terms and some men served more than once, making it difficult to arrive at a figure that correctly expresses the size of the armies. If the number is expressed as the equivalent of men serving three-year enlistments, the Union army had in all about 1,500,000 in its ranks and the Confederacy, 1,000,000. Even official figures are confusing, but approximately 360,000 men of the North and 258,000 men of the South died, including the very considerable number who succumbed to disease. If the surviving wounded of both sides are added, the war took a toll of more than 1,000,000 casualties. In addition, of course, the destruction of property in the South was very great. One estimate puts the value of southern property at the end of the war, not counting slaves, at not much more than half what it was in 1861. Finally, no one can measure the sorrow visited upon mothers and fathers, wives and sweethearts, on both sides by the loss forever of so many young men who were willing to die for a cause.

# 6 Behind the Armies

THE CIVIL WAR did not consist only of the clash of armies. Victory or defeat also depended on governmental organization, the procurement of supplies and equipment, finances and civilian morale. Although a basic organization existed in the framework of the Federal government, it was not geared to centralized control of the nation's resources. The American ideal of individualism and local authority was at odds with the concept of an all-powerful central government. The situation had to be altered if hundreds of thousands of armed men were to be put in the field. In the same way, the nation's industrial and transportation systems, although expanding every year, had to grow even faster and produce better management systems.

Part of the problem, to be solved by trial and error and by decisions of Congress and of President Lincoln, was the question of the extent of the powers of the Federal government in wartime. The Constitution, for example, says that the right of habeas corpus cannot be suspended "unless when in Cases of Rebellion or Invasion the public Safety shall require it," but it does not say who has the power to effect the suspension. The purpose of a writ of habeas corpus is to release a person from unjust imprisonment, and when Lincoln declared the right suspended, his authority to do so was challenged in the courts. After a Maryland secessionist was imprisoned by the army in 1861,

Chief Justice Taney ruled that only Congress could suspend the right of habeas corpus. Lincoln ignored the ruling and justified his action in a message to Congress. Two years later, Congress ratified the president's right to take the action he had.

By the end of 1862, Lincoln also had troubles within his own party. The fall elections that year gave evidence of considerable dissatisfaction with the way the war was going, and the Democrats made wide gains, even in Lincoln's own state of Illinois. Then came the defeat at Fredericksburg on December 13. Four days later, a delegation of senators called on Lincoln and demanded that he reorganize his cabinet, getting rid of Secretary of State Seward and giving Secretary of the Treasury Chase the most important place in the body. The senators represented the Radical Republicans, who were growing in strength and who were also firm abolitionists, intent on seeing the slave-owning class punished. They believed Congress, not the president, should determine the terms under which the southern states would be readmitted to the Union when the war was won—and those terms would be harsh. The radicals were also political opportunists who saw the war and its aftermath as offering a chance to elevate the Republican party and destroy the Democrats.

Among the leaders of the Radical Republicans were Charles Sumner (1811-74) and Thaddeus Stevens (1792-1868). Sumner had been in the Senate since 1851 and was chairman of the foreign relations committee. While a very intelligent man, Sumner was arrogant and had little personal warmth. He held that by seceding, the southern states had "committed suicide" and so had lost all their rights. Stevens, of Pennsylvania, had served in the House from 1849 to 1853 and returned to it in 1859. He was chairman of the powerful ways and means committee. A founder of the Republican party, he thought of the southern states when the war ended as "conquered provinces."

The Radical Republicans made it clear to Lincoln that they

distrusted Seward, and that the price of their cooperation was a cabinet dominated by radicals. Lincoln, however, refused to dismiss Seward and the radicals received little open support from members of the cabinet except Chase. The radicals could do nothing more and so the crisis subsided.

The Confederate government, although it took over some of the machinery of the Federal government in its area, had to start almost from scratch. The organizers of the new government were, in addition, strong supporters of states' rights and looked with suspicion on any attempt of the central government to add to its powers. Yet in a war situation, more centralization than ever was necessary. President Davis, unlike Lincoln, was not an effective political leader and was unable to communicate successfully either with the people of the South or the other leading political figures.

For the Confederacy, the problem of financing the war proved too much in the end. The South had no substantial banking system and southerners were not accustomed to paying heavy taxes, while the blockade meant that customs duties were mostly unavailable. Taxes levied upon the states resulted in those units borrowing or issuing paper money to pay the taxes. When a comprehensive tax law was passed in 1863, it called for an income levy and a tax of ten percent in kind on farm products. This was highly unpopular. The Confederacy also tried borrowing money from its citizens and from abroad, and in all raised over $700,000,000, but this source dried up in time. Like most governments in such circumstances, the Confederacy resorted to printing paper money, and issued more than $1,500,000,000. As the South declined both in finances and in military position, this paper money became almost worthless. By the fall of 1863, butter cost $4 a pound; a few months later potatoes were $25 a bushel; and by the end of the war a barrel of flour cost $1,000 in Richmond.

At the start of the war, the South pinned its hopes on cotton, both for financing and to attract the support of the European powers, especially Great Britain. "Cotton is King" was the slogan. In the preceding years, as the demand for cotton grew, so had production in the South. Prewar peaks were reached in 1860 and 1861 with 3,841,000 bales and 4,491,000 bales respectively. At the start of the war, some states and some individuals attempted to prevent the export of cotton to Great Britain in the belief that that country would need cotton so badly it would come to the aid of the Confederacy to obtain some. England, however, had a large supply on hand and could get more from Egypt and India. It was, in fact, much more in need of northern grain than of southern cotton. When the northern blockade became effective, the South had no way to secure funds by selling cotton abroad. Cotton production declined, partly because there was no market and partly because the land was needed to grow food crops. Only 299,000 bales of cotton were produced in 1864, and it is estimated that during the war about 2,500,000 bales were destroyed, either by the South to keep it out of Union hands or by northern troops because they could not move it. A sizable amount of cotton was seized and moved north as Union armies advanced.

For a good part of the war, the North walked a tightrope in its relations with Great Britain and France. Trouble began as early as November 8, 1861, when a navy ship, the *San Jacinto*, commanded by Charles Wilkes (1798-1877), stopped a British ship, the *Trent*, and removed from it two southerners who were on their way to Europe to represent the Confederacy. These commissioners were James H. Mason (1798-1871), who had represented Virginia in the Senate from 1847 to 1861 and had drafted the Fugitive Slave Act of 1850, and John Slidell (1793-1871), who was born in New York and later became a prominent citizen of New Orleans. He served in the Senate from 1853 to 1861. Wilkes brought the men to Boston and was a popular hero.

He had, though, acted in violation of international law and Great Britain threatened war. A British note, presented December 31, was fortunately softened by Prince Albert, the prince consort. Seward, meanwhile, was seeking a way out. His reply admitted that Wilkes should have brought the ship as well as the men to port for adjudication, and consequently the United States would release Mason and Slidell, who proceeded on their way as commissioners to London and Paris respectively.

Upper-class English citizens tended to side with the Confederacy. They had business and social ties with the South and believed the southern planters were more like the British landed gentry than were the people of the northern states. Conservatives among them would also have been happy to see democracy curbed on the other side of the Atlantic, and men of this type were largely in control of the British government. Several groups in England, however, were favorably inclined toward the Union. Manufacturers had valuable commercial ties with the North, while the strong British humanitarian movement—antislavery and prodemocracy—supported the Union. Leaders of the labor movement also favored the North.

Although Great Britain never officially recognized Mason's mission on behalf of the Confederacy, the South at first made some diplomatic gains. In addition to issuing a proclamation of neutrality and recognizing the South as a belligerent, England allowed warships to be built in its shipyards for the Confederate navy.

Defending the interests of the North was an unusually able diplomat, Charles Francis Adams (1807-86), son of the late President John Quincy Adams. He carried on a diplomatic battle with the British government until finally, in September 1863, that government seized some ironclad ships under construction and refused to let them or any more vessels be produced for the Confederacy. When northern victories indicated the cause of the South was doomed, and when the Union began taking steps to end slavery, public opinion in Britain swung more to the North, and the Confederacy lost all chance of aid or recognition.

Napoleon III, emperor of France, was more friendly toward the South than was the British government, but he dared not act on his own so far as aiding the Confederates. In January 1863, he proposed that North and South accept him as a mediator to try to settle the war, but Seward at once rejected his proposal. After Great Britain stopped the building of Confederate ships in its territory, Napoleon agreed to allow four cruisers to be built in France. When Seward protested, Napoleon backed down and only one such ship ever served the South.

As far as Lincoln and his administration were concerned, the war at first was not fought to free the slaves but to reunite the nation. As soon as Union armies entered the slave territory of the seceding states, however, the problem of handling slaves arose. Until August 1861, escaping slaves were treated as contraband, on the basis of the earlier cabinet decision. At that time, Congress passed the First Confiscation Act, which applied only to slaves who had been employed against the United States. The Second Confiscation Act of July 1862 freed the escaped slaves of any master who was disloyal to the Union. During this time the Fugitive Slave Act of 1850 was still legally in effect, but its enforcement ended for practical purposes. Congressional action in April 1862 abolished slavery in the District of Columbia, with compensation to be paid to owners, and in June another law ended slavery in the territories. The administration in this same period negotiated a treaty with Great Britain for more effective suppression of the African slave trade.

Lincoln came under increasing pressure from the Radical Republicans and others to take more steps toward ending slavery. Horace Greeley, in his New York *Tribune* on August 20,

1862, addressed an open letter to the president, claiming that the whole North wanted sterner action. Lincoln was happy to have an opportunity to state his position and he wrote Greeley, in part:

> My paramount object in this struggle is to save the Union, and is not either to save or to destroy slavery. If I could save the Union without freeing *any* slave I would do it, and if I could save the Union by freeing some and leaving others alone I would also do that.

The favorable response of moderates to Lincoln's statement indicated that Greeley did not speak for everyone and that many people did not consider immediate abolition desirable.

Lincoln was against slavery but faced the practical problem of holding the border slave states. He also had his own ideas as to how and when emancipation might be accomplished, and his plans called for compensated emancipation and for colonization of the freed blacks in Africa or Latin America. Lincoln proposed such a scheme to the state of Delaware, but it was rejected. He went further in his message to Congress in December 1862 by proposing a constitutional amendment which would give states until January 1, 1900, to free all slaves. The states would pay the owners and in return would receive Federal government bonds. Near the end of his message, he said:

> In giving freedom to the slave, we assure freedom to the free. . . .
> We shall nobly save, or meanly lose, the last, best hope of earth.

Nothing came of the president's proposals.

Earlier in the year, however, Lincoln had decided on the one step that symbolically, at least, made the Civil War one for ending slavery as well as reuniting the country. In July he read to his cabinet an Emancipation Proclamation he proposed to issue on January 1, 1863. Because the military situation was unfavorable, his cabinet urged him to delay any announcement of his plan. Lincoln waited until September 22, when Lee's invasion of the North had been halted by the battle of Antietam, to announce the proclamation, which he justified under the general war powers he often appealed to. When issued at the start of the new year, the Emancipation Proclamation actually freed slaves only in territory still under the control of the Confederacy. Thus it did not affect blacks in the border states or in southern territory occupied by Union forces. In short, it freed the slaves where Lincoln had no power to enforce the proclamation and left them slaves where he did. The proclamation did not do anything in practice that acts of Congress had not already accomplished.

For this reason it was denounced by extreme abolitionists and, for other reasons, denounced by the Confederacy. Even some northerners objected to having the war turned into one against slavery. On the whole, though, there was much rejoicing for the symbolic action and for what it had to mean in terms of practical measures in the future.

Another matter of more immediate concern to the two governments was that of keeping up or increasing the strength of their armed forces. At the start of the war, both sides relied on volunteers and had no difficulty securing as many men as they could outfit and train. The South was the first to pass a conscription law, in April 1862. This called for service by all white men between the ages of eighteen and thirty-five. In a few months the upper age limit was changed to forty-five, and in 1864 the age limits became seventeen and fifty. The law had loopholes, including the one that allowed a man to hire a substitute. Most objectionable was the provision that exempted one owner or overseer for every twenty slaves. To the poorer classes this made it "a rich man's war and a poor man's fight."

The North did not have a conscription act until March 1863. This act made men twenty to forty-five years of age liable for military service. A man could, however, not only provide a substitute, he could also evade service simply by paying $300. A very unpopular law, it led to disturbances in a number of places, but chiefly in New York City in July. Here the cause of a riot lasting several days was not just the law itself. At the time, the longshoremen—many of whom were Irish-Americans who tended to be sympathetic to the South—were on strike and employers had hired blacks as strike breakers. When some of the strikers were drafted, rioting broke out. Many blacks were beaten to death, an orphanage for black children was burned, along with other buildings, and an armory was seized. Troops had to be rushed from Meade's army to quell the riot and this weakening of his forces contributed to his failure to pursue Lee after the battle of Gettysburg. In all there were about 1,000 casualties. After that the draft functioned but never contributed significantly to the total of the Union forces.

Lincoln's administration also had to deal with northerners who opposed the war in such a manner that some people thought they were guilty of treason. Called "Copperheads" both because they cut the head of the goddess of liberty from copper pennies to wear in their lapels, and for the venomous snake, they were mostly Democrats and were particularly strong in Ohio, Indiana and Illinois. The Copperheads were chiefly interested in attacking Republican rule, and in turn, the Republicans used their pro-Confederacy acts as an excuse for condemning the whole Democratic party as being disloyal to the Union. The secret arm of the Copperheads was an organization called the Knights of the Golden Circle, organized as far back as 1854 to aid proslavery interests. It was reorganized in 1863 as the Order of American Knights and the next year as the Order of Sons of Liberty.

At its peak, somewhere between 200,000 and 300,000 persons belonged to the order. Its leader during the war was Clement L. Vallandigham (1820-71), an Ohio lawyer who was strong for states' rights and served in the House from 1858 to 1863. In May of 1863, after a speech in which he charged the war was really being fought to free the blacks and enslave the whites, General Burnside had him arrested and court martialed. He was sentenced to prison for the rest of the war, but Lincoln, showing his sense of humor, commuted the sentence to banishment to the Confederacy. Vallandigham escaped to Canada, and while there was the 1863 losing candidate of the Peace Democrats for governor of Ohio. The next year he returned to the United States and was unmolested.

Both sides tried their best to provide adequate care for the sick and wounded, but without much success. To some extent this was caused by the general ignorance as to the causes of infection and disease. The South, in addition, was short of medical supplies because of the blockade. To augment the government services, private citizens in the North organized the United States Sanitary Commission, which raised $25,000,000 to provide bandages, medicine, clothing, food and tobacco to Union soldiers and to wounded Confederates in Union hands.

In the days when men ran most activities, two women played major roles in the care of Union wounded. Clara Barton (1821-1912), who had been a teacher and a government clerk, organized nursing services at the start of the war and later was in charge of the search for missing men and the task of identifying unmarked graves, as at Andersonville Prison. Dorothea Dix (1802-87), who already had a national reputation for her work in the reform of prisons and institutions for the mentally ill, was appointed superintendent of women nurses of the Union forces in June 1861.

Four months after the crucial battle of Gettysburg, on November 19, 1863, a ceremony was held on the battlefield to dedicate the cemetery in which lay dead soldiers of both the North and the South. Invited to deliver the principal address was Edward Everett (1794-1865) of Massachusetts, who had been president of Harvard University and secretary of state. The most noted orator of the day, he had stirred crowds across the land with his speeches in support of the Union. On this occasion he spoke for two hours, delivering a well-thought-out speech. President Lincoln was then scheduled to make a few remarks, which he did in the space of three minutes, concluding

> . . . that we here highly resolve that these dead shall not have died in vain; that this nation, under God, shall have a new birth of freedom; and that government of the people, by the people, for the people, shall not perish from the earth.

Comments of listeners and of newspaper editors were mixed. Many praised Everett's speech and criticized Lincoln's Gettysburg Address, now generally thought to include some of the most moving words ever uttered.

When 1864 came, and with it the time for another presidential election, Lincoln did not think his chances were very good because of public dissatisfaction with the progress of the war. He was renominated with little opposition at the Republican party (also called for war purposes the Union party) convention, but the Radical Republicans were against him and Secretary Chase indicated he thought he should have the nomination. Horace Greeley, most influential of editors, was also strongly anti-Lincoln. Just at this time, too, the Union army under Grant seemed to be bogged down before Richmond and the war news, in general, was depressing. Disaffected Republicans even went so far as to call another convention for late September for the purpose of replacing Lincoln on the ticket. Then came better news from the fronts: victory of Mobile Bay, Sherman's capture of Atlanta and Sheridan's victories in the Shenandoah Valley.

The opposing party was split between War Democrats and Peace Democrats. In effect, the war group named the candidate when the convention chose General McClellan, while the other wrote the platform. This platform favored the end of hostilities and the restoration of peace on the basis of reuniting the states, but how this was to be done was not clear. McClellan ignored the point about ending hostilities and campaigned as a war leader who could do a better job of winning the war and reuniting the states. In the election in November, Lincoln had a wide margin in the electoral college, 212 to 21, but the popular vote was much closer: 2,216,000 to 1,808,000.

Shortly before Lincoln's first term ended he agreed, on the basis of feelers put out by the South, to a meeting to discuss ending the war. The conference was held on February 3, 1865, on board the Union transport *River Queen* in Hampton Roads. Lincoln and Seward represented the Union, Vice-President Stephens and two others acted for the Confederacy. Lincoln presented his terms: emancipation of the slaves, the immediate disbanding of the Confederate forces and reunion of the states. The Confederacy refused these terms and so the conference achieved nothing.

When Grant launched his final campaign against Lee and Richmond and when the southern capital fell in early April, Davis and his cabinet fled south. Davis was captured and imprisoned on May 22 in Fortress Monroe, where he was held for two years. Although charged with treason, he was released from jail and the case was never pressed. At Christmas 1868, a general pardon freed the only Confederate president of all charges.

Lincoln delivered another of his memorable and moving speeches at his second inauguration on March 4, 1865. At the close he said:

> With malice toward none, with charity for all; with firmness in the right, as God gives us to see the right, let us strive on to finish the work we are in; to bind up the nation's wounds. . . .

Meeting with his cabinet on April 14, Lincoln told its members that he hoped there would be no persecution of the defeated. That night, while attending the theater, he was shot in the head. He died the next morning. His assassin, John Wilkes Booth (1838-65), was an actor, son of another prominent actor, Junius Brutus Booth, and a Confederate sympathizer. He had first planned to kidnap the president, then decided to assassinate him. Booth was cornered in a barn on April 26 and killed by those seeking to capture him. Four persons were hanged for their part in the conspiracy, including Mrs. Mary E. Surratt (1820-65), in whose boardinghouse Booth had plotted. Samuel A. Mudd (1833-83), a physician who set the leg Booth broke when he leaped from the president's box onto the stage, was sentenced to life imprisonment although he had no part in the plot. He was pardoned in 1869.

At his death, Lincoln was beginning to be recognized by the mass of the people as a great man, as "Father Abraham," who had brought them through four terrible years. At the beginning of his presidency, many thought him well-intentioned but lacking in leadership; others believed he was simply weak and indecisive. To some, he was too tenderhearted, as shown in his pardoning of deserters; to the South he was a brutal baboon. Lincoln himself said: "My policy is to have no policy." His enemies said this showed he didn't know where he was going, but what he meant was that he was realistic, dealing with problems in a practical way as they arose, rather than making solutions fit preconceived theories or ideologies. In this approach, as in his compassionate nature, he fitted the ideal of the American leader.

Even before his death, Lincoln had had to deal with the problem of Reconstruction—how to treat the southern states as the Confederate forces were driven out of them—and it was apparent that he and the Radical Republicans did not see eye to eye. Now a new president would have to face the problem.

# 7 Reconstructing a Nation

WHEN UNION troops drove the Confederate forces out of all or most of a seceded state, a new civil government had to be established under northern auspices. Lincoln had no definite plan as to the best way to do this, but did assume that he would decide the matter as part of the war powers of the president. He refused to get involved in theoretical questions as to the status of the seceded states. Three days before he was assassinated, he summed up his point of view by saying that those states were "out of their proper practical relation with the Union" and that the object of his efforts was to get them back into a proper relation.

Lincoln first outlined a plan to reconstruct the rebellious states on December 8, 1863. All Confederates would be pardoned who swore to support the Constitution of the United States. If ten percent of the number of voters who had cast ballots in the 1860 election took such oaths and established a state government that abolished slavery, Lincoln would consider that state back in the Union. Governments were established under this plan in Arkansas, Louisiana and Tennessee, but their validity was questioned and Congress refused to allow representatives and senators named by these governments to take their seats.

Congress tried to take a hand in Reconstruction in July 1864, when it passed the Wade-Davis Bill, named for its chief sponsors who were two of the most extreme of the Radical

Republicans. Benjamin F. Wade (1800-78), senator from Ohio, was a strong abolitionist and chairman of the congressional committee on the conduct of the war, the activities of which had been merely meddlesome. Henry W. Davis (1817-65) was a representative who helped greatly in keeping Maryland in the Union. The Reconstruction bill sponsored by these men required more than half the white male citizens of a state to take an oath to the Constitution, swearing they had never been disloyal. After that a state government could be organized, providing slavery was prohibited and any state debt incurred for the Confederacy repudiated. No one who had held a Confederate office or had fought against the Union voluntarily could vote. Lincoln killed the bill with a pocket veto, although he said that if any state wished to reorganize under this system he had no objection. The two men retaliated by issuing the Wade-Davis Manifesto, a violent attack on Lincoln and his motives.

Lincoln's death changed the situation, just as the war was ending in April 1865. His successor to the presidency was Andrew Johnson (1808-75), a native of North Carolina who had lived most of his life in Tennessee. A tailor by trade and a self-educated man whose wife had taught him to write, Johnson went into politics early in life and spent most of his career in one public office or another. By 1857 he was in the Senate, and in a few years was the only southern senator to support the Union. Lincoln appointed him military governor of Tennessee in 1862, when that seceding state came largely under Union control, and Johnson did well in the post. As a southerner and a Democrat, but unmistakably loyal to the Union, he was a practical political choice for the vice-presidency on the ticket with Lincoln in 1864.

By the time Johnson became president, the situation in the South was desperate. Farms, city buildings and factories had been devastated in many areas and the railroads were mostly inoperable. Banks had failed, the state governments were near collapse and their credit was exhausted. In addition, the population was both angry and dejected at the result of the war. Prompt action was needed and Johnson proposed to act, both because he believed Reconstruction was an executive, not a legislative function, and because Congress would not meet until December 1865. Johnson's plans at first pleased the radicals because they treated the South more severely than Lincoln's. His proclamation of May 29 disenfranchised all military and civil officers of the Confederacy and anyone who owned property worth more than $20,000. Johnson, coming from a background of poverty, showed here his lifelong dislike of the planter class. He proceeded to appoint provisional governors of the seceded states. These governors were to call conventions, the delegates to which must take a loyalty oath, and the conventions were to set up new state governments. Ordinances of secession were repealed and slavery abolished. By December, every Confederate state except Texas had satisfied Johnson's formula and so far as he was concerned, Reconstruction was almost complete.

During this process, little was done either by Johnson or the new state governments to help the former slaves. Johnson never believed in equal rights for blacks while the new state governments, despite the loyalty oath, were under the control of former slaveholders, the same kind of men as ruled before the war. In short order the southern states established Black Codes, laws varying in harshness, but all intended to control the Negroes. With the slave and master relationship ended, the blacks were free to go their own way, but they were not accustomed to the responsibility of managing their own affairs. Accordingly, some took to wandering and showed no desire to work. Even for those who wanted to work, no pattern was yet set to govern the changed relationship with their former masters. The codes did give blacks the right to marry, to own personal property and to sue in court. Beyond that, however, they restricted the blacks' right to own real estate; specified the occupations they were allowed to pursue; and segregated public facilities. Vagrancy laws were strict. The North, especially the radicals, saw these codes as intended to reenslave the blacks.

In the course of 1865, the Federal government did take two steps in aid of the blacks. One was the passage of the Thirteenth Amendment to the Constitution, which abolished slavery, a legal step that was necessary even though slavery was dead as a practical matter. Johnson made ratification of the amendment a requirement of the new southern state governments and it was proclaimed a part of the Constitution on December 18, 1865.

Of more practical importance was the establishment of the Freedmen's Bureau in March 1865, and extended until 1869 the next year, in a law passed by Congress over Johnson's veto. The bureau, with offices all over the South, provided food and financial assistance for blacks (and also for whites), tried to secure justice for the blacks and see that their labor was not exploited. It also administered abandoned and confiscated property. The bureau's best work was in the field of education, where it established some 4,000 schools with nearly 10,000 teachers, most of them from the North. Some of its work was excellent; in other areas it was inefficient and some of its employees were corrupt. The chief commissioner of the bureau was Oliver Otis Howard (1830-1909), a Union general who had lost his right arm at the battle of Fair Oaks. He was dedicated to his work, although he was not too efficient as an administrator.

When Congress reassembled in December 1865, there was much feeling in Washington and, indeed, throughout the North, that Johnson's Reconstruction policies were too lenient and that the South must be punished. Although they did not hold a majority in Congress, the Radical Republicans were able to dominate proceedings. They formed the Joint Congressional Committee on Reconstruction (usually known as the Joint Committee of Fifteen because it consisted of nine representatives and six senators). When the committee reported in April 1866, it declared the Johnson-sponsored state governments were not valid, partly because they did not protect the civil rights of blacks. From then on, Congress and Johnson were completely at odds.

The Radical Republicans put a Civil Rights Act through Congress that same month, and passed it over Johnson's veto. This act gave citizenship to the blacks and the same civil rights as anyone else. Three more Civil Rights Acts, attempting to insure equal treatment in public places, the right to serve on juries and covering other matters, were enacted in 1870, 1871 and 1875.

In the spring of 1866, the Joint Committee of Fifteen proposed a Fourteenth Amendment to the Constitution, the chief purpose of which was to establish the citizenship of blacks and to deny states the right to abridge any privileges of citizenship. One reason for this provision was to ensure the constitutionality of the Civil Rights Act. Among other clauses was one declaring the Confederacy's debts void, and another designed to keep former Federal officials who had served the Confederacy from regaining office without the consent of Congress. President Johnson let it be known he opposed the amendment, which further widened the gap with the radicals. The amendment seemed doomed when by March 1867 twelve of the states, including all the seceded states except Tennessee, rejected it. The next year, another law made ratification a requirement for readmission to the Union, and the amendment was declared in effect on July 28, 1868.

The 1866 fall election was a clear fight between Johnson and the radicals. A speaking tour Johnson undertook, during which he acted in an undignified manner and spoke intemperately, alienated many people. The Republicans claimed credit for winning the war and asserted only they could bring the unrepentant South to its senses. The Republicans won more than two-thirds of the seats in both houses of Congress and from then on the radicals held full control of the course of Reconstruction.

An act of March 2, 1867, and subsequent amendments to it, declared presidential Reconstruction unsatisfactory and made the southern states, except Tennessee, start all over. New constitutions had to be written, which provided for Negro suffrage and which disqualified former Confederate leaders. The South, in the meantime, was to be divided into five military districts with a Federal army officer and troops holding superior power over the states. President Johnson vetoed the Reconstruction Act and Congress at once overrode his veto overwhelmingly. By mid-1868, six states—Alabama, Arkansas, Florida, Louisiana, North Carolina and South Carolina—satisfied Congress's terms and were readmitted to the Union. It was two more years before the other four—Georgia, Mississippi, Texas and Virginia—qualified.

The southern state governments established under the Reconstruction Act caused much controversy, and in some areas this led to violence. A large number of northerners went south to take part in the Reconstruction process. Southerners sneered at them as "carpetbaggers," the implication being that they could carry all their possessions in a piece of hand baggage. Some of the carpetbaggers were able and sincere people who wanted to help the blacks; some hoped to make their fortunes in the reconstructed South; some were crooks. Also participating were southern whites who had not been members of the former, and now excluded, ruling class. They were labeled "scalawags" by the latter. The blacks, unprepared for participation in government, were thrust into politics.

Unreconciled southerners tried to paint a picture of complete—and corrupt—control of the state governments by ignorant blacks. Actually, South Carolina was the only state in which blacks controlled the legislature and no black was governor of any state. Only two black men, both from Mississippi, were elected to the United States Senate, and only fifteen served in the House. There was some corruption and some of it was on a large scale, but corruption was fairly common in the North at this time, too. Charges that the radical-inspired governments spent money on an enormous scale were not generally true either, considering what needed to be done. Taxes had to be increased and money borrowed to get various services functioning again. State governments loaned money to repair railroad systems, for example, and some of this money found its way into the pockets of promoters and government officials. Public school systems free of segregation were established for the first time in the South's history.

This was an unhappy period at best. The majority of the white southerners were angry in defeat, the blacks in many cases did not know how to cope with their new status and the Radical Republicans were intent on using the situation to perpetuate their own rule. Union League Clubs, formed in the North beginning in 1862 to support the Republicans and the war, moved their activities to the South. Through carpetbaggers and scalawags they tried to make Republicans of the blacks, reminding them that the party had set them free. Thaddeus Stevens, for example, said the blacks must have the vote because "on the continued ascendancy of that [Republican] party depends the safety of this great nation."

One of the southern answers to such activities was the 1866 formation of the Ku Klux Klan, which spread through the South, and had half a million members or more. Men on horseback, in white robes and hoods, terrorized Negroes especially, but also carpetbaggers and scalawags. Whippings and lynchings were not uncommon in this attempt to counteract the Union League Clubs and to cause the breakdown of the radical Reconstruction state governments by driving the blacks out of political life. The Grand Wizard, or commander, of the Klan was Nathan

Bedford Forrest (1821-77), who at the end of the war had been a lieutenant general in command of all the Confederate cavalry.

When the radicals started their own Reconstruction plan, they also began a vindictive campaign to curtail Johnson's powers and to drive him from office. A major step was the passage, over Johnson's veto, of the Tenure of Office Act on March 2, 1867. This law forbade the president to remove any Federal officeholder who had been appointed "by and with the consent of the Senate" without Senate approval. It also provided that cabinet members would serve for the term of the president who appointed them, plus one month. The purpose of this clause was to prevent Johnson from removing Secretary of War Stanton, who was on the radicals' side and who controlled the troops stationed in the South under the Reconstruction Act. Since Lincoln, not Johnson, had originally appointed Stanton, it would seem the law did not apply, but when Johnson dismissed the war secretary, who refused to give up his office, the radicals seized on the action as an excuse for impeaching the president. A committee drew up eleven articles of impeachment, but they all boiled down to Johnson's defiance of the Tenure of Office Act.

The House voted impeachment on February 24, 1868, and in early May the trial began in the Senate. Participating in the trial was the president pro tem of the Senate, Senator Benjamin F. Wade, who would become president of the United States if Johnson were convicted. Some thought it unethical, if not illegal, for Wade to take part under these circumstances, but he did so and voted for conviction. On May 16 the Senate balloted on one of the articles of impeachment and on May 26 on two others. In both cases the tally was thirty-five to nineteen, one vote short of conviction, since a two-thirds majority was required. Seven Republicans voted with twelve Democrats against convicting Johnson. The radicals then dropped the matter.

After Johnson left office in 1869, two more major efforts were made to protect the southern blacks by legislation. The

Fifteenth Amendment, which said the right to vote could not be denied "on account of race, color or previous condition of servitude," was proposed in 1869 and declared ratified on March 30, 1870. The former Confederate states soon found ways of getting around the amendment and, in fact, the situation was little better in the North. In 1867, for example, the voters of Ohio, New Jersey and Maryland rejected Negro suffrage. Between 1870 and 1875 four Force Acts were passed, all intended to strengthen the enforcement of the Civil Rights Acts and the Fourteenth Amendment.

In spite of the radicals' zeal and the many ways they used the government to prop up the southern state governments which they sponsored, those governments were short-lived. White planters, lawyers, merchants and small farmers joined forces, and by persuasion and intimidation drove the blacks and the scalawags from politics. Between 1869 and the summer of 1876, these conservative groups—called Redeemers—took back control of the governments in all the former Confederate states except Florida, Louisiana and South Carolina, and they, too, soon after fell in step. At the same time, the wartime radical leaders were passing from the scene and most of the North was growing tired of the struggle, feeling little real sympathy for the blacks. Reconstruction was over.

# 8 The General as President

MUCH OF the attention of Congress, the president and the nation at large, not only during President Johnson's term of office but also during General Grant's eight years in the White House, was focused on Reconstruction, but not to the exclusion of all other matters. Even as the radicals were taking Reconstruction out of Johnson's hands in the spring of 1867, Secretary of State Seward was negotiating the peaceful purchase of territory one-fifth the size of the continental United States. Russia took the initiative in offering to sell Alaska, 586,400 square miles of almost unknown land in the far northwest of the continent and Seward, always a strong expansionist, lost no time in concluding a treaty. The United States agreed to pay $7,200,000, and the Senate quickly ratified the necessary treaty. Even though the House took until mid-1868 to agree to the necessary appropriation, the American flag was raised over what many called "Seward's Folly" or "Seward's Icebox."

The eyes of expansionists also roamed over both the Pacific Ocean and the Caribbean Sea. In the Pacific, the Midway Islands, a group of small isles 1,150 miles northwest of Hawaii, which had been discovered by the United States in 1859, were annexed in August 1867. That fall Seward negotiated a treaty with Denmark, which wanted to sell the Danish West Indies (now the Virgin Islands), but the Senate foreign relations committee took no action and so the matter ended.

Relations with China were stabilized and improved as a result of the work of Anson Burlingame (1820-70), a diplomat and former congressman. He was sent to China as American minister in 1861. His tact and his conduct, so unlike the autocratic and condescending manners of other foreign diplomats there, made such a favorable impression on the Chinese that they asked him to act for them as head of a mission to visit European countries and the United States to gather information and negotiate treaties. He did this successfully, including the signing of the Burlingame Treaty (1868) he negotiated with the United States. This treaty did not treat China as an inferior nation, as the European nations tried to do, gave Chinese and Americans the right to travel and reside in the others' country, and pledged the United States not to interfere in Chinese domestic affairs.

Once the Civil War was over, the United States was free to put an end to an adventure in empire-building in Central America that had disturbed it for some time. Great Britain, Spain and France staged a military demonstration in 1862 to try to collect overdue debts from France. All but France went no further, but Napoleon III, vainly wanting to emulate his conquering uncle, Napoleon I, sent French troops to occupy Mexico City in 1863. He then prevailed upon Maximilian (1832-67), an Austrian archduke, to allow himself to be crowned emperor of Mexico in 1864. The United States protested on the grounds that this invasion was a violation of the Monroe Doctrine of 1823, which stated that the United States would not allow any European nation to secure control of any country in the Americas. By February 1866, Seward was in a position to give the French an ultimatum to get out or face General Sherman and 50,000 American troops. Napoleon agreed to withdraw his soldiers but delayed until June 1867. As soon as the French soldiers were gone, the Mexicans seized Maximilian and executed him. His wife, Carlotta (1840-1927), daughter of King Leopold I of Belgium, escaped. Her mind gave way under the strain of events but she lived on for sixty years.

As Johnson's term of office came to an end, it was clear that neither the Republicans nor the Democrats would nominate him. Grant, the greatest northern military hero of the war, was acceptable to the Radical Republicans and was unanimously nominated on the first ballot. The Republican platform appealed for support chiefly on the grounds that the party had saved the Union and freed the slaves. For the rest of the century the party waved the "bloody shirt of rebellion" in election campaigns. The platform endorsed radical Reconstruction, called for the Federal debt to be paid off in gold, but was unclear as to where the party stood on black suffrage. The Democrats, after twenty-two ballots in search of a candidate, nominated Horatio Seymour (1810-86), a former governor of New York State. He had been a strong critic of Lincoln, said the Emancipation Proclamation was unconstitutional and opposed military conscription. The Democrats in their platform condemned radical Reconstruction and pledged to pay off the national debt with paper money. In the election, Grant's victory by 214 to 80 electoral votes was not nearly so overwhelming as it seemed. Three of the southern states were not allowed to participate and six others were controlled by radical governments. Grant received 3,015,000 popular votes, but this was only 306,000 more than Seymour. Since about 450,000 blacks voted, mostly for Grant, it appeared to observers that Seymour received more votes from whites than did Grant.

Besides the problems of Reconstruction, Grant's new administration in 1869 also inherited the continuing argument with Great Britain over the Union's claim to compensation for the damage done shipping by the Confederate raiders built in Great Britain. A treaty was at last signed in 1871, in which

England expressed regret and agreed to arbitration over damages. The following year a commission of one American, one Briton and three neutral Europeans awarded the United States $15,500,000. Thus the "Alabama Claims" question, growing out of the depredations of the Confederate raider *Alabama* and similar ships, was settled peacefully.

Early in his administration, a group of land speculators was able to interest Grant in trying to acquire the island of Santo Domingo in the Caribbean. Ignoring the State Department, the president sent his secretary, Orville E. Babcock, to the island to look into the matter. Babcock came back with a treaty in 1870 and Grant did his best to force annexation through the Senate by means of the treaty, or by a joint resolution of both houses of Congress, but Congress would have none of it.

As in this instance, General Grant was naïve in dealing with unscrupulous promoters and businessmen, and was completely without experience in practical politics. To his misfortune, he had entered the White House at a time of growing corruption in both government and business. The "spoils system," whereby appointment to government posts depended almost entirely on which political party was in control, had fastened itself on the government machinery over the years. The war, with its opportunities for enormous profits in selling goods to the government, had resulted in much profiteering and, in many cases, in close alliances between businessmen and public officials for the monetary benefit of both. As a result, the nation was on the verge of entering an era that came to be called appropriately the "Gilded Age," in which corruption flourished and in which those who suddenly became wealthy enjoyed making a vulgar display of their affluence. Reformers in politics and in newspapers and magazines made enough clamor for reforms that Congress in 1871 passed a bill establishing a Civil Service Commission, and authorized the president to make rules for hiring personnel for public service. Grant appointed George William Curtis (1824-

92), an editor and reformer, as chairman. When the commission's recommendations were completely ignored, both by Grant and by Congress, Curtis resigned in 1875.

The worst scandal of Grant's first administration began in 1868, before he even took office, but did not come to light until 1872. This concerned a company known as the Credit Mobilier of America, and a number of public officials, mostly members of Congress. The Credit Mobilier was formed by the promoters of the Union Pacific Railroad, which was to build part of a transcontinental line. The directors of the railroad then awarded construction contracts to the Credit Mobilier, and these contracts produced enormous profits that went into the promoters' pockets. To make sure Congress did not intervene, the company "sold" some of the stock to members of Congress at very low prices. The scandal was exposed in the fall of 1872 and in February 1873, one representative, Oakes Ames (1804-73), who had carried out most of the dealings between the company and members of Congress, was censured by that body. Others implicated, but who neither explained their connection nor were punished, included the vice-president of the United States, Schuyler Colfax (1823-85) and James A. Garfield, a future president.

Largely as a result of such scandals and because of Grant's subservience to the Reconstruction plans of the radicals, many leaders of the Republican party were dissatisfied with the general and did not want him renominated in 1872. They formed the Liberal Republican party, and in convention adopted a platform calling for civil service reform, withdrawal of troops from the South and payment of the national debt in specie. When the new party tried to nominate a candidate for the presidency, however, it found that its various elements were united in being against various things but otherwise were an assortment of discordant groups. None of the logical candidates could poll enough votes and the party finally settled on Horace Greeley

(1811-72), the nationally known editor of the New York *Tribune* for thirty years. The Democrats, attracted by the Liberal Republicans' opposition to radical Reconstruction and the hope of defeating Grant, reluctantly adopted Greeley as their candidate also. The Republicans renominated Grant on the first ballot.

The ensuing campaign was one of the oddest in American history. Greeley had always been impulsive and unpredictable, and had championed any number of fads and movements. He was both a visionary and, in the eyes of some, a figure of fun. Many Democrats, remembering his attacks on their party over the years, refused to vote for him. As a result, Grant won by a larger margin than before. Greeley carried only six states, none of them in the North. Grant received 3,597,000 popular votes, 763,000 more than his opponent, and 186 electoral votes to Greeley's 66. Greeley, brokenhearted by his defeat and by the recent death of his wife, died less than a month after the election.

Scandals of one kind and another continued. William A. Richardson (1821-96), Grant's secretary of the treasury, was censured and forced to resign in 1873, after an investigation showed that contracts he had let for the collection of taxes had resulted in the Treasury being defrauded. Nevertheless, in 1874 Grant appointed Richardson to the United States Court of Claims—an example of his blindness to what people expected of a president. About the same time, the "Salary Grab" affair aroused national indignation. Early in 1873 Congress passed a bill that not only increased the salaries of members of Congress by fifty percent, but also made the increase retroactive for two years. Even though this latter aspect of the bill seemed clearly to violate the Constitution, Grant signed it without questioning it. The public outcry was such that in January 1874, Congress repealed the law so far as it applied to the salaries of its members.

The temper of the country was revealed in the mid-term elections of 1874, when eighty-five seats changed hands in the House of Representatives. The Democrats took control of the

House for the first time since the start of the war while Republican control of the Senate was weakened.

The Democrats in the House began a number of investigations, one of which uncovered an extreme example of corruption in government. This was the "Whiskey Ring," a group of distillers, chiefly in St. Louis, and corrupt Treasury Department officials who had conspired to defraud the government of millions of dollars in taxes on liquor. The ring was broken up by the energetic prosecution of the secretary of the treasury, Benjamin H. Bristow (1832-96), a lawyer and Union officer in the Civil War. He secured 238 indictments, among them that of Grant's secretary, Orville E. Babcock. Although Grant said: "Let no guilty man escape," he intervened to make sure Babcock was not convicted, although 110 others were. Grant also forced Bristow out of office in June 1876.

In foreign affairs, Grant's second term was marked by the *Virginius* incident. A ship by that name, trying to smuggle arms to the Cubans who were in revolt against Spanish rule of the island, was captured in 1873 by the Spaniards. The captain and some of the passengers and crew, totaling fifty-three persons, were executed. Some of the victims were American citizens, and it also turned out that the ship was flying the American flag fraudulently. The incident brought Spain and the United States close to war, but a settlement was negotiated in which Spain agreed to pay $80,000 in damages. Here and in the matter of the Alabama Claims, the calmness and diplomacy of Secretary of State Hamilton Fish (1808-93) were invaluable. Fish, who had been a senator from 1851 to 1857 and had originally been a Whig in politics, served through Grant's two terms and was one of the few outstanding men the general appointed to high office.

The Supreme Court in 1873 ruled in a significant case, one of the first to involve the post-Civil War amendments to the Constitution. The state of Louisiana in 1869 granted a twenty-five-year monopoly to one slaughterhouse on the grounds of protecting the public health. Other slaughterhouses sued, claiming that they had been deprived of their property without "due process of law," as stated in the Fourteenth Amendment. The court decided that although the amendment could not be considered to concern Negro rights only, it did not include rights such as those in question. It was not the intent of the amendment, the Court continued, to transfer power over all civil rights from the states to the Federal government. The decision was a conservative one, since it slowed, temporarily at least, the postwar movement toward centralizing more power in Washington.

Radical Reconstruction and Grant's career as president came to sorry ends at approximately the same time. Reconstruction had caused nothing but trouble, both in the North and the South, and everyone was tired of struggling with it. The general had demonstrated that he had no talent for politics or governmental administration. He seemed to have lost his resoluteness and had become a poor judge of people, appointing to office friends who betrayed him. The victor on the battlefield had been defeated by the presidency.

# 9 The West: Farmers and Ranchers

HAD THERE been no Civil War, the assault on the western prairies and mountains by farmers, ranchers and miners could well be considered the most dramatic aspect of American history in the quarter-century from 1850 to 1875.

In the course of the 1850's, the prairie farmer, settling in the rich, almost treeless land of the upper Mississippi Valley, became the typical American farmer, replacing the earlier agriculturalist who settled in wooded areas. During the decade, more than 2,200,000 people were added to the populations of Illinois, Iowa, Indiana and Missiouri—with the first two of these states, on opposite sides of the Mississippi, gaining the most. Illinois's growth was greater than that of any other state in the Union and 67,000 new farms were begun there. In all, nearly 600,000 new farms, totaling 114,000,000 acres, were first plowed in this decade, bringing the nation's total to 2,000,000 in 1860. During the same period, the value of farmland went up by more than $3,000,000,000, a 100 percent increase. This growth could not have been so great had it not been for the spreading railroad network, which not only helped bring new settlers to the land—both Americans and immigrants—but also provided a means of getting the increased volume of agricultural products to market.

The expansion of western farmland, added to the not inconsiderable acreage already being worked in the East and the

South, meant an amazing growth in total production. It resulted in yields of 838,800,000 bushels of corn, 172,600,000 bushels of oats and 173,100,000 bushels of wheat in 1860. The wheat figured importantly in foreign trade. Great Britain bought 24,500,000 bushels in the year ending June 30, 1861, to make up for its own bad harvest. An increase in milk products was encouraged by an extension of the milkshed area made possible by the railroad, and fruit production was encouraged by the growth of commercial canning, which expanded the market during the 1860's from 5,000,000 to 30,000,000 cans. Beginning in the 1860's, the horse began to replace the plodding oxen as the chief beast of burden on farms, but there were 2,255,000 oxen at that time. Sheep raising spread quickly across the country.

The war increased the demand for farm products, but the Union had no great problem as output in the loyal West continued to rise. The farm population grew during the war in spite of the drain to the armed forces. Some people, in fact, went west to farm to avoid the war, and immigration from Europe continued. Only in the case of horses and mules did the war put a drain on northern and western farmers. The Federal government purchased more than 500,000 horses and 250,000 mules. In the South the situation was different. Planters there had regularly bought food products from the West, keeping most of their own acreage in cotton. Now this supply was cut off, and as the war went on, the production of sufficient food to feed the army and the civilian population became a serious problem. The value of northern farms continued to increase during the war while southern agricultural property fell in value.

By the time the war ended, the states just west of the Mississippi were moderately well settled. So, too, was the West Coast area and spots in the adjacent mountains that attracted miners. Between lay the Great Plains, the one remaining unsettled area. In the late 1860's, farmers began to move into this region, slowly at first, but by the mid-70's land was being taken up in areas where in some years there was not enough rainfall for farming as practiced further east. Many experts believed the 97th meridian, running through eastern Kansas and Nebraska, was the western limit for farming, but others claimed that "rain follows the plow"—that for some unknown reason farming would increase the rainfall.

This treeless, semiarid flatland demanded new solutions to the problems of pioneering. With no trees for lumber, settlers built sod houses. These consisted of strips of sod, usually about sixteen inches wide, that were laid on top of one another like bricks to make the walls. Usually the floor was the earth and sometimes the house was partly underground. Sod was used for roofing also. Water was scarce and wells were dug, one man doggedly going down 300 feet with pick and shovel. Sunflowers became popular because their dried stalks made good firewood, and so, too, did buffalo chips until the buffalo disappeared. A special stove was designed to burn hay efficiently. Natural disasters were on a grand scale, such as a prairie fire on a 100-mile front that burned everything in front of it in Kansas in 1869. A horde of grasshoppers swept through Dakota Territory, Nebraska and Kansas and on down to Texas in 1874. A column 100 miles long and 150 miles wide ate everything in sight, including horses' harnesses, window curtains and plow handles, and their bodies made railroad tracks so slippery locomotives could not run. In bad years, many settlers gave up the struggle with the Great Plains, but others came to take their places.

One factor in the growth of the West was the Homestead Act of 1862. Attempts had been made for several years to pass a law that would give public land free to settlers, but the South disapproved of the Federal government giving away public land. The Republicans promised the western agricultural interests, and those in the East who wanted land for surplus industrial workers, that it would enact such a bill, and when the South seceded it did. The law gave to anyone over twenty-one, who was a citizen or going to become one, or the head of a family, 160 acres of land if the person settled on it for five years and then paid a nominal fee. If settlers wished to acquire title earlier, they could do so after six months by paying $1.25 an acre. In the first year, 1863, 8,223 homesteads were taken up, and by the end of the war the total was 26,552. Then the pace increased, with 15,355 homesteads spoken for in 1866 and 39,768 in 1871. As much of a boon as the Homestead Act was to the approximately 2,000,000 people who found new homes under it, it contributed only in a rather small way to the overall settlement of the West. Land was available to settlers from other sources, especially from the railroads whose grants from the government often included better land, and land which totaled far more acres.

Another Federal law intended to aid western pioneers on the prairies was the Timber Culture Act of 1873. People eligible under the Homestead Act could secure another 160 acres if they planted a quarter of the area in trees in ten years' time. A later amendment reduced the amount to one-sixteenth. This attempt to foster a moisture-saving process was only moderately successful.

While the prospects of western agriculture seemed ever brighter, the South in this quarter-century went through a period of decline caused by the war and the problem of reviving an agricultural economy on the basis of free labor instead of slave. Even so, production recovered quite rapidly considering the devastation of the war. Cotton production, down to 299,000 bales in 1865, bounced back to 2,094,000 the following year and to 4,631,000 in 1875. Only 18,000,000 pounds of cane sugar were produced in 1865, compared with 459,000,000 in 1861, but the total in 1870 was 144,000,000. The tobacco crop was half again as big in 1875 as it had been in 1860.

A fundamental change did, of necessity, take place in the economics of southern agriculture. As a result of the freeing of

the slaves, and the damage caused by the war, some large plantations were broken up—although not as many as might have been
expected. Many planters were land-poor, having large acreage
but no labor force and no cash. The blacks, for their part, were
inexperienced in their new relationship to the planters. Some
Union generals during the war and the Freedmen's Bureau later
tried to provide blacks with their own land but little came of this.
In the meantime, plantation owners were trying to hire back
their former slaves, or other blacks, to produce cotton as before.
Many owners tried by these means to control again the lives of
the blacks, and others cheated them, usually through the
amounts they deducted for living costs. Dissatisfaction resulted
and sometimes the whole work force of a plantation disappeared
overnight.

By the late 1860's this gang labor system was collapsing,
partly because the owners had little cash with which to pay wages
while a crop was being produced. Out of this situation grew the
sharecropping system. The sharecroppers were engaged to
grow cotton, or some other crop, on a given number of acres of
plantation-owned land. The usual arrangement was that if the
croppers supplied only labor, they received a third of the crop. If
they also provided the essential draft animals, seed, equipment
and other necessities, they received two-thirds. The arrangement could also call for some other division, depending on who
supplied what, but in most cases the black sharecroppers had
only the labor of themselves and their families to offer. Local
storekeepers entered the picture a little later because they could
advance supplies of food, fertilizer and other items for which
neither the landowners nor the croppers had the cash or credit.
It was not a very efficient system of farming, nor did it give the
croppers much chance to put money aside to buy their own land
eventually.

Although pioneer farmers are pictured as ideal American
individualists, they often, especially in the Middle West, found it

worthwhile to organize for self-protection. The National Grange of the Patrons of Husbandry was founded in 1867. The leading organizer was Oliver H. Kelley (1826-1913), who had farmed on the Minnesota frontier and worked in Washington for the Bureau of Agriculture. In the beginning, the Grange was a social and educational organization, but it soon got into politics. Expanding rapidly after the Panic of 1873, the Grange reached a peak of 858,000 members in 1875. Its chief political enemies were the railroads and the owners of grain storage elevators, which often were also railroad companies. The Grangers claimed that exorbitant and discriminatory freight rates were charged and that elevator and warehouse owners used their monopoly position to squeeze the farmer. As a result of Granger pressure, a number of states, beginning with Illinois, passed laws to control and limit railroad rates and grain storage charges.

Numerous advances in agricultural technology and science made farming somewhat easier and increased the productivity of farm acreage. One basic improvement was the chilled-iron plow (1868). The sulky plow, which enabled the farmer to ride behind the team, was first devised in 1844 but was not fully successful until about twenty years later. A reaper that delivered grain on a flat surface where two workers could bind it was patented in 1858, and nearly doubled the amount that could be harvested in a day. By 1864, the farms of the North and West were using about 250,000 reapers and mowers. Other improvements being perfected were the horse rake, the thresher and a wire binder. On the prairies, where fencing material was scarce, the patenting in 1874 of a process for making barbed wire solved this problem. Now whole cattle ranges could be fenced in. Within a year, 600,000 pounds of barbed wire were sold. The Department of Agriculture was established in 1862, although it was not at first given cabinet rank, and by 1866 it had twenty-nine employees.

Ranching as well as farming underwent great growth and change, especially after the war. Since the days of Spanish rule, cattle raising had been carried on on a large scale in Texas. With the increase in the urban population of the North and the extension of rail lines across the Mississippi, ranching began to enjoy its best days and expanded all over the Great Plains. One important event was the discovery that cattle could stand the northern winters, and so the ranchers' domain spread all the way to the Canadian border. For two decades, ending in the late 1880's, ranchers, cowboys and cattle roamed over this expanse of flat land.

The culmination of the rancher's year was the roundup and the drive to the railheads. The cattle were driven in herds of about 1,000 each, with half a dozen cowboys and a trail boss keeping them on the trail. About a quarter of the cowboys after the war were blacks. The drives followed such trails as the Chisholm, named for Jesse Chisholm, a part-Cherokee Indian trader who initially drove his wagon from Texas through Indian territory in the spring of 1866. The first of a number of towns that became famous as railheads where cattle arrived from the ranches for shipment east was Abilene, Kansas, described in 1867, the year of the first such drive, as "a very small, dead place." It did not remain that way long. Between 1867 and 1871 a total of 1,460,000 cattle arrived in Abilene and with them hundreds of cowboys, lonely and with money to spend. Such towns as Abilene provided them with opportunities to relax and get rid of their wages.

Among the legendary ranchers who built up some of the largest ranches were Richard King (1825-85) and Charles Good-night (1836-1929). King, born in New York, made a fortune during the Civil War by running cotton from Texas to Mexico through the Union blockade. When he founded his ranch in 1853, it consisted of 75,000 acres. By the time he died he had expanded it to 500,000 acres between the Nueces River and the

Rio Grande. Goodnight was from Illinois and was a Texas Ranger and Indian fighter before becoming a rancher. In 1866 he laid out the Goodnight Trail for cattle from Texas to Wyoming, and by 1877 he possessed a ranch of nearly a million acres and 100,000 head of cattle.

The size and scope of the westward movement in the United States in the nineteenth century cannot be matched elsewhere. A growing native population, plus increasing immigration from Europe, demanded more land to live on. The Homestead Act and other laws, plus the need for more cattle and foodstuffs to feed the urban population, encouraged the opening of new farm and grazing lands. In addition, some years of bad harvests in Europe and a number of wars there accelerated the demand for food, especially wheat.

# 10 The West: Miners and Indians

THE FIRST settlers in parts of the West, especially in the mountains beyond the Great Plains, were miners. They and the farmers and ranchers not only settled the West, each in his own way, but together with the railroad builders brought about the final showdown between the white and the American Indian civilizations.

The discovery of gold in California in 1849 started a boom in mining that in the following years spread north and south and east. As early as 1852, California gold production reached its peak of 81,295,000 ounces and began to decline. Some miners settled down as farmers, but other restless ones set out for new areas in which to prospect. Mining at the same time was becoming an industry requiring special knowledge, heavy machinery and capital supplied from the East.

Nevertheless, independent prospectors discovered the greatest source of gold and silver of all, the Comstock Lode, although it was discovered and rediscovered several times, beginning in 1857, before its true extent was realized. The Comstock Lode is in western Nevada, on Mount Davidson. Its name came from a lazy, shiftless man, Henry T. P. Comstock, who talked himself into a partnership with some others who held one of the claims staked out in 1859. Comstock eventually sold out for $11,000. Everyone was looking for gold, and it was not until unusually rich silver ore was found and recognized that the Comstock Lode became a great bonanza. In a period of twenty years, $300,000,000 in gold and silver was taken out of it, not by individual miners with pick and shovel, but by the use of machinery and the drilling of deep shafts and tunnels.

Typical of the few who struck it rich in mining were the four men who became the chief beneficiaries of the Comstock Lode. James C. Flood (1828-89), born in Ireland, and William S. O'Brien (1826-78) of New York City went to California in the rush of 1849. Both tried mining without much success and then turned to storekeeping. They became partners in a saloon in 1857 and their contacts with customers gradually took them into the stockbroking field. This resulted in their meeting James G. Fair (1831-94) and John W. Mackay (1831-1902), who were already speculating in mining claims in the Comstock area. Fair and Mackay were both Irish-born, and like the other two had been drawn to California by the gold rush. By astute business dealings, these four gained control of mining companies and claims that returned them millions of dollars. Flood and Fair built showy mansions, but O'Brien, who was worth $12,000,000 when he died, never lived as though he were rich. Fair served as senator from Nevada, while in the 1880's Mackay turned his attention to a company that laid telegraph cables to Europe.

The discovery of the Comstock Lode also led to the founding of Virginia City, Nevada, one of the most luxurious and exciting cities in America at its height. It never had more than 35,000 inhabitants, but besides hotels, restaurants and jewelry stores to match anything New York could offer, Virginia City also had 110 saloons. The first newspaper in Nevada was established there in 1861, and one of its reporters a few years later was a promising young author named Mark Twain.

Colorado had its gold rush in 1859 in the Pike's Peak country, and also near Denver. Word of a strike spread east (there were rumors of Arapaho Indians who fired golden bullets) and

100,000 would-be miners, mostly from the Mississippi Valley, began the journey westward. About half turned back before reaching the mining area, but enough went on to make a small city out of Denver, which by 1860 had a theater, a circulating library and a debating club. Gold was found in the Columbia River in Washington Territory in 1854, but an uprising of Yakima Indians halted any rush. Miners fanned out over southern Idaho in 1860 and on east into Montana. Later, discoveries of silver and lead drew other miners to Idaho. Farther east in the Black Hills of Dakota Territory, gold seekers rushed in after gold was reported there in 1875. One result of this rush was the founding of Deadwood, South Dakota, which became famous for the number of desperados who supposedly hung out there. The graves of Deadwood Dick and others can be seen. These first mining efforts provided a colorful touch to American history. Only a few people struck it rich, most turned to other pursuits, and in time large companies took over and used modern methods and machinery to extract the valuable ores.

Another colorful part of the history of the West concerns the people, horses, wagons and stagecoaches that, before the railroad network was complete, provided transportation for people, goods and the United States mail. Wells, Fargo and Company was founded in 1852 to operate express service between New York and California, using trains as far beyond the Mississippi as they then went, and going the rest of the way with horsepower. Wells, Fargo carried east most of the gold and silver the miners found, and for about twenty years provided almost all the postal service for the mining camps. For some time after 1854, the slower freight business of the West was dominated by Russell, Majors and Waddell, a concern formed late in 1854, with Leavenworth, Kansas, as headquarters. The company hired 1,700 workers and purchased 7,500 oxen and 500 wagons. The wagons could carry loads of 5,000 pounds and were hauled by a dozen oxen each.

More glamorous than freight hauling was the Pony Express, another enterprise of Russell, Majors and Waddell. This service began in April 1860, extending from St. Joseph, Missouri, to Sacramento, California. The 2,000-mile route was covered in eight days by riders on horses, traveling some of the way through hostile Indian territory. Stations were set up ten to fifteen miles apart where riders changed horses. The service was expensive— a half-ounce letter cost $5 to send—and the service lost a great deal of money. It was also doomed to a short life when the completion of the transcontinental telegraph line in October 1861 made its service much less attractive. An earlier system for reaching the Pacific Coast faster than by ship was the Butterfield Overland Mail, established in 1858. Mail and passengers traveled 2,800 miles, from Tipton, Missouri, to San Francisco, over a route that looped far south before heading north. The trip took twenty-five days, the mid-part, in unsettled territory, being made in light "celerity wagons" rather than stagecoaches.

As early as the 1840's, the Indians of the many tribes spread over the Great Plains and through the Southwest began to show hostility toward the white settlers who were encroaching on the trans-Mississippi west and journeying across the Great Plains to California and Oregon. There were about 225,000 Indians in the area at this time. Attempts were made to pacify the Indians by treaties and promises, and there were relatively few clashes until the Civil War period. The Indians' way of life was threatened by the growing slaughter of the bison, on which they depended for food and other necessities. An estimated 10,000,000 bison still roamed the plains in 1865, but by 1890 they were gone except for 1,000 or so. They were shot for sport and by professional hunters. Usually all that was considered worth salvaging was the hide (worth about $2.50) and the tongue, which became a gourmet delicacy and sold for 50 cents.

By mid-century, the Federal government's policy was to negotiate with the Plains Indians to try to protect the growing number of settlers. When the Department of the Interior was created in 1849, the Indian Office was moved over from the War Department. The Indian Appropriation Act of early 1851 provided funds to expand the work of the office, and $100,000 to negotiate treaties, the purpose of which would be to move the Indians to reservations. In the fall of 1851, government agents persuaded about 10,000 Indians from a number of tribes to leave emigrant wagon trains alone and to stay in areas assigned to them. Each tribe was to get $50,000 a year for ten years for this, and was to be protected from attacks by whites. Twelve treaties in which Indians gave up 18,000,000 acres to the government were signed in 1854 alone. This policy resulted in forcing the Indians into a settled agricultural life, which Plains Indians did not like or understand. One treaty that same year, with the Omaha Indians, allowed the president to divide up all or part of the tribal land among individuals of the tribe who wanted to settle in a permanent home. The final goal of such a plan was to assimilate the Indians, which to most whites meant Christianizing them and breaking up the tribal system.

After the Civil War the increased pace of westward migration and railroad building added to the friction between whites and Indians. A Federal Peace Commission, consisting of distinguished civilians and army officers, was appointed in 1867 and visited the West. It recommended, and Congress agreed, that the process of negotiating treaties, as though dealing with a sovereign, foreign power, be abandoned in favor of simpler forms of agreement, but otherwise nothing much came of its work.

The general corruption of Grant's administration and the chicanery associated with the dealings of government officials with the Indians were joined in the case of William W. Belknap (1829-90). Belknap had been a Union general in the war and was appointed secretary of war in 1869. Evidence came to light in 1876 showing that he had indirectly received bribes from the official trader at one of the Indian posts. Belknap was impeached and resigned. The Senate did not convict him because some of the members believed they had no jurisdiction once Belknap had left government office.

Fighting between whites and Indians grew more frequent as time went on. From 1869 to the late 1870's, more than 200 pitched battles were fought, and even then the last shot had not been fired. Small units of the army, stationed in posts scattered over the West, were responsible for keeping the peace, but faced many difficulties. Before the Civil War, most of the troops were infantry and therefore were no match for the mounted Indian warriors. In any event, there were too few of them, and in many instances the Indians had more modern arms than the army. Also, while the government guaranteed the Indians certain territory, it did nothing to keep settlers out of such territory. After the war, General Sherman was put in command in the West. Sherman thought too much was being spent to protect scattered settlers, who should give up their exposed positions. Settlers, on the other hand, felt the army spent more time protecting the railroads and their workers than it did the settlers and the trails they used.

In the Southwest, the Navaho, Comanche and Apache Indians all fought the whites. The power of the Navahos was destroyed in the winter of 1863-64 when Kit Carson (1809-68), noted frontiersman and scout, led a force that trapped the Navahos in a canyon which they had converted into a stronghold. The Americans seized the Navahos' flocks and herds, destroyed their gardens and cut down their peach trees. The entire tribe was placed on a reservation in northeastern Arizona and never fought the whites again. Quannah Parker (c. 1852-1911), son of a Comanche chief and a white woman, became chief of his father's tribe in 1867. His mother, Cynthia Ann Parker (c. 1827-64), had been captured at her father's trading post when she was about nine. When recaptured by whites in

1860 she wanted to rejoin the Comanches. Parker led many raids against the Americans until 1875, when he saw the inevitability of Indian defeat. He surrendered, adjusted to white ways, promoted education and agriculture, and at one time was believed to be the wealthiest Indian in the United States.

The Apaches fought the longest in the Southwest, mostly under two chiefs, Mangas Coloradas (c. 1797-1863) and Cochise (c. 1815-74). Mangas Coloradas had first fought the whites, then had been friendly with them until 1851, when a group of miners humiliated him by flogging him. From then on he waged war against the whites until he was captured and killed by Union troops in 1863. Cochise, too, had been friendly to the Americans but he turned against them when soldiers hung some of his relatives for crimes they had not committed. From then on he waged a relentless war, showing great courage and considerable military skill. In 1872 his friendship with a white man led him to lay down his arms and accept peace terms. The worst event of the bloody war between the Apaches and the whites was the Camp Grant Massacre in 1871. A group of about fifty civilians from Tucson, together with a hundred Papago Indians, attacked an Apache reservation near Camp Grant, killing 108 Indians, of whom only eight were men. They also captured twenty-nine children. The perpetrators were indicted but the Arizona jury would not convict a white person for killing an Indian.

To the north and on the central plains, the Sioux and the Cheyenne Indians waged war with the invading whites. The Sioux rose up in Minnesota in 1862, indignant at their treatment by settlers and by government agents. They killed more than 800 settlers before General Pope and his Union troops, intended for the Civil War battlefronts, captured 1,800 of them. Of these, 303 were condemned to death by hanging, but Lincoln commuted the sentences of all but thirty-eight.

Black Kettle (d. 1868) was the chief of the southern

Cheyenne in Colorado and tried to make peace with the United States. In 1864, though, his tribe was attacked at Sand Creek by some volunteers, not army troops, who slaughtered and mutilated hundreds of men, women and children even though Black Kettle raised a white flag. He signed agreements with the government in 1865 and again in 1868 and might have persuaded his people to settle on reservations. Army troops in November 1868, however, fell upon the tribe in the battle of Washita River, killing Black Kettle and most of his followers. These troops were under the command of George A. Custer (1839-76), who, in 1863, had been the youngest general in the Union army, but had now reverted to his regular rank of lieutenant colonel. In 1874 Custer led a force into the Black Hills of South Dakota, an area that by treaty had been reserved to the Sioux Indians as sacred ground. Custer thought gold would be found in the area, and when this proved correct, he let the fact be known. A rush followed that found 15,000 prospectors in the region by the fall of 1875 and, in turn, further warfare with the Sioux was the result.

In Wyoming and Montana, the Oglala Sioux, led by Chief Red Cloud (1822-1909), also fought to protect territory promised to them. In the winter of 1862-63, John M. Bozeman (1835-67), a gold seeker, blazed a trail to the Montana mining fields, a shortcut that branched off from the Oregon Trail. But the Bozeman Trail, as it became known, ran through lands reserved to the Indians. Nevertheless, it became popular, and in 1865-66 the government built three forts to protect it. The Indians took to harassing those using the trail and the troops guarding it. Their greatest success came in November 1866, when William J. Fetterman (1833?-66), who had been cited for gallantry in the Civil War and was now stationed at Fort Kearny, volunteered to lead a party on supply escort duty. Knowing nothing of Indian warfare, he ignored orders not to leave the trail. His force was ambushed by Indians under Red Cloud and all eighty were killed. Bozeman was also killed by Indians in 1867. The government was forced to give up any pretense of protecting the trail and for practical purposes it was abandoned. Red Cloud agreed to live in peace with the government, but he was suspected of encouraging hostile Indians.

The Red River War of 1874-75 was the last fought on the southern plains, seven years after the Peace Commission of 1867 had placed the tribes on reservations. Ill-treated and short of rations, the Indians were also unwilling or unable to raise any crops of their own, and when buffalo were scarce they took to raiding settlers' herds. By fighting the Indians the year-round instead of stopping for the winter, troops under General Sheridan broke the Indians' resistance and they returned to their reservations.

The Indians of the Far Northwest were for the most part subdued in wars fought in 1854-55 and 1872-73. The earlier trouble stemmed from the activities of Isaac I. Stevens (1818-62), who became governor of Washington Territory in 1853. He was also superintendent of Indian affairs there. Stevens was anxious to clear the way for railroad building and settlers and miners, and so he tried to force the various tribes around Puget Sound and in the interior to cede their lands and live on reservations. His tactics of coercion and fraud caused the tribes to revolt, but by 1858 they were all defeated and most of their chiefs killed or hanged.

One of the most protracted battles occurred in the black lava beds near Tule Lake, California, where a band of Modoc Indians took refuge late in 1872 after leaving their reservation. Under their chief, Kintpuash (d. 1873), who was called Captain Jack by the whites, they held out until May 1873. In the course of the war, the Indians killed two government peace negotiators and the army brought up 1,000 troops in all. When the Indians surrendered, Captain Jack and five others were hanged.

These were by no means all the massacres and battles in

which whites and Indians participated, nor was this the end of the bloodshed. By 1875, however, the inevitable was clear: the Indians were being drastically reduced in numbers; their power to harm the miners, the farmers, the ranchers and the railroads was about to end; and they were doomed to life on government reservations.

# 11 Cities, Immigrants and Nativists

As HAD been true earlier and would be for many years to come, the quarter-century from 1850 to 1875 showed an increase in the urbanization of the United States. This was caused in part by the continued migration to this country of large numbers of people, ranging from 92,000 to 460,000 annually during the period. Urbanization and immigration—combined with industrialization—set off a reaction on the part of Americans of older stock against foreign influences which, they feared, would mean the end of the American way of life as they saw it and thought it should be.

In 1850, 15.3 percent of the population lived in urban areas. By 1860 this proportion was up to 19.8 percent; by 1870, 25.7 percent; and by 1880, 28.2 percent. Most of the urban areas were in the North and East, although the midwestern cities were growing more rapidly and small cities were springing up overnight in the trans-Mississippi west. The South was far less urbanized than the North, with only 7.2 percent of its people living in places of 2,500 or more in 1860, and having only fourteen of the ninety-three cities with populations of more than 10,000. Three American cities in 1860 had populations exceeding 200,000: New York, 813,000; Philadelphia, 566,000; and Baltimore, 212,000. Another six, including Brooklyn, then a separate city, counted more than 100,000.

That industrialization and the consequent spread of transportation facilities were major factors in making cities grow was shown particularly in the Midwest. Pittsburgh was the center of the steel industry; Cleveland was both a lake port and the first center of the new petroleum refining industry; Chicago was both a port and the railroad hub of the nation with fifteen trunk lines entering it by 1868; Minneapolis grew because it was a great flour milling center. As examples, Cleveland's population increased from 17,000 in 1850 to 93,000 in 1870 and Chicago's from 30,000 to 299,000.

Even more spectacular, in a comparative way, were the new cities of the Great Plains and mountain areas that were founded in this period. They were often laid out, settled and growing while the surrounding territory had hardly any population. Denver owed its growth to mining and later to the fact that a railroad was built to connect with the new transcontinental line but the site had been chosen first by real estate speculators. The same kind of men decided where Wichita, Kansas, was to be. In 1872, two liquor dealers learned where the new railroad line would run west of Fort Dodge, and became the founders of Dodge City. Cheyenne, Wyoming, began as the casually chosen site of a railroad construction camp in the summer of 1867, and by fall had a population of 4,000. On the Pacific Coast, San Francisco, already made into a busy city by the gold rush, prospered still more as its railroad connections grew, and by 1869 it had 159,000 people. Obviously, not all pioneers took up farming.

As the cities grew in population they spread outward, and as they spread, mass transportation became a problem. It was solved for a time by the introduction of cars drawn by horses along rails laid flush with the streets, an invention of the late 1840's. New York's horse railways carried nearly 35,000,000 passengers in 1858, and by 1866 there were sixteen different lines, using 800 cars and nearly 8,000 horses. Philadelphia, with

148 miles of such railways, had more mileage than any other city. Mass transit was speeded even more, but at the cost of additional dirt and noise, by the building of elevated railroads. The first was started in New York in 1867 and completed in 1870. Even with elevateds, street traffic was so congested that a magazine noted in 1874: "How to cross Broadway is one of the problems of life in New York."

Public health was also an urban problem because municipal services did not keep pace with population growth and because there was a lack of knowledge of the causes of various diseases. Of the nation's cities in 1860, 136 had city water systems but only ten had sewage disposal systems. New York City in 1857, for example, had only 158 miles of sewers for 500 miles of streets. A Metropolitan Board of Health was established in 1866, and after that the city cleaned up its streets, finally getting rid of the hogs that had roamed at will. Other cities were also taking action, but Cincinnati in the 1860's, with fifty slaughterhouses, had to put up with about half a million hogs trotting through the streets every year. Epidemics took high tolls. Yellow fever in the 1850's killed 25,000 people in New Orleans, and there was a large-scale cholera epidemic in 1866, spread mostly through water contamination.

Police and fire protection was improved and became professionalized. Philadelphia established a central police force in 1850; New York, in 1853, for the first time required its force of 800 to wear uniforms; while Boston organized a department of 250 in 1854. Cincinnati, in 1853, was one of the first cities to have a paid fire department and many others soon followed, but New York did not do so until 1865. At this time, too, steam-powered pumpers were replacing the old hand pumps. It was a time of devastating fires all over the country, with flames sweeping through the wooden city blocks. Portland, Maine, suffered a $10,000,000 fire that destroyed 1,500 buildings in July 1866, while a large part of St. Louis was destroyed in May 1851. The most ravaging of all, though, was the Chicago fire in October 1871, started, according to legend, when Mrs. O'Leary's cow kicked over a lantern. The fire raged for two days, destroying about 17,500 buildings spread over 2,000 acres and doing $200,000,000 damage. About 98,000 people were made homeless and several hundred were killed. Chicago began to rebuild at once.

As the cities grew and as more poor immigrants poured in, the slum areas increased. After about 1860, each ethnic group tended to live in its own section of a city and these became slum areas. Those who made good and moved to better locations were replaced by newcomers. By the 1850's in New York, buildings were being built especially to house the poor and the word tenement came to be applied generally to any residential building in a slum area. A new building at the time was described as five stories high, thirty-four feet wide and running 234 feet back from the street. This building housed 500 people, with no plumbing or heat. Ten years later, its population had increased to 800. A count in 1864 showed that 15,511 tenements, some better and some worse than this one, housed about 500,000 people out of a total New York population of over 800,000. Crime was on the increase in cities and many people blamed it on the immigrants and the slum residents. One of New York's upper-class citizens, a resident of the fashionable Gramercy Park area, said, in 1857, that most of his friends were buying revolvers for self-protection.

While American cities were getting larger, noisier and dirtier and seemingly more unhealthful, some people began to agitate for more planning and control of urban development and for provision for some amenities that would take at least a bit of the harshness out of city life. Thus by the 1860's the value of parks within cities was acknowledged and the first steps taken. One of the earliest of these, Central Park in New York City, proved to be one of the finest examples. It encouraged other cities to plan their own parks, and brought fame to its designer, Frederick Law Olmsted (1822-1903). Olmsted was already fairly well-known as a journalist for the very observant books he wrote about the slaveholding society of the South as a result of trips to the region. When Central Park was proposed, it was fought by real estate interests and politicians, but by 1858 Olmsted's far-reaching and far-seeing plans for it were accepted and he was appointed landscape architect for the project. The genius of his finished work was recognized and Olmsted spent most of the rest of his life designing other parks and park systems: in Brooklyn, Buffalo, Boston, Chicago and other places.

Corruption in government reached the municipal level in many places. Philadelphia suffered from a crooked Republican political machine. In New York, which had the biggest civic scandal of all, it was the Democratic organization, Tammany Hall, that provided the culprits. The Tweed Ring, as it became known, took its name from William Marcy Tweed (1823-78), an ingratiating figure who worked his way up the political ladder until he gained control of the city through the Democratic machine. He and his associates robbed New York of somewhere between $30,000,000 and $200,000,000 by way of padded bills and kickbacks on contracts for new buildings, for cleaning streets and for other services.

The ring's downfall began in July 1871, when *The New York Times* printed evidence of corruption. Tweed's candidates were badly beaten in the election that fall. The attack on Tweed and his friends was aided by Thomas Nast (1840-1902), an illustrator and painter whose Civil War drawings in *Harper's Weekly* brought him wide attention. His savage cartoons aroused people against the Tweed Ring and it was he who created the tiger, the elephant and the donkey as the symbols of Tammany Hall, the Republican party and the Democratic party. Modern political cartooning began with Nast. Also prominent in the fight against Tweed was Samuel J. Tilden (1814-86), a successful lawyer and

Reform Democrat who turned up some of the evidence used to prosecute the ring. His work helped to elect him governor of New York State in 1874 and to secure him the Democratic nomination for president in 1876. Tweed was arrested and convicted in November 1872, but after serving only a year, he was released. When arrested on other charges, he fled to Spain, from which he was extradited and jailed again. He died in jail in 1878.

During this period, not all immigrants settled in American cities, but a very large number did and they contributed even more to urbanization than to the total population. In the quarter-century, 6,640,000 people from foreign countries, mostly in Europe, arrived in the United States. Of this total, 2,598,000 came in the prewar decade. Between 1861 and 1870, the number dropped slightly, to 2,315,000. In the five years, 1871-75, 1,727,000 more reached American shores, an annual rate higher than in the two previous decades. The two years of lowest migration were the first two years of the war, but 1863 immigration almost doubled that of 1862. More immigrants—459,803—came in 1873 than in any other single year in the quarter-century. Almost one out of every five persons in the country was of foreign birth by 1875.

Most of the immigrants came from the British Isles (Ireland in particular), Germany, Scandinavia, Holland and Switzerland. By 1855, 469,000 of New York State's inhabitants were Irish-born and 218,000 German-born. The number of Jews emigrating to the New World began to increase, the Jewish population growing from 50,000 in 1850 to 150,000 in 1860. Most Jewish immigrants at this time were German-speaking. The immigrants came for a variety of reasons: to better themselves economically; because of political or religious persecution; because of dislocations caused by industrialization; and, finally, because railroads, steamship companies, industrialists and some western states enticed them with promises of land and jobs.

The immigrants settled mostly in the North and east of the Mississippi, the Irish in the seaboard cities in large numbers. Cincinnati became a center of German and German-Jewish culture, while other Germans and many Scandinavians went still farther west as pioneer farmers. Only half a million foreign-born persons lived in the slave states in 1860. Immigrants avoided the area not necessarily because they disliked slavery, but because the South offered them no job opportunities or ways to acquire land in comparison with the free states.

The government did little either to control or assist new arrivals. Congress passed a law in 1855 intended to protect immigrants from overcrowding and unsanitary conditions on shipboard, but it was not well enforced. The same year, at Castle Garden, a building in lower Manhattan, a depot was established to receive the newcomers. During the war, active recruiting was carried out at Castle Garden, with bounties offered for immediate enlistment. Some immigrants became soldiers almost as soon as they stepped on American soil and in all about 500,000 foreign-born men served in the Union army.

The steady arrival of a large number of immigrants was a major cause of the growth of nativism—a dislike of everything foreign and an unrelenting defense of everything "American." In practice, this meant all persons and institutions that were not Protestant and Anglo-Saxon were suspect. Beginning in the 1840's, the movement reached its peak in the first half of the 1850's. Opposition to the Roman Catholic Church was nativisim's most obvious trait. This, in turn, made the Irish leading targets of the nativists. When a papal nuncio from the Vatican was sent to the United States in 1853 to settle some problems that had arisen within the Church, nativists rioted against him as a representative of reactionary Europe and the forces that had suppressed Italian freedom fighters in 1848. The Irish were accused of corrupting American politics, although they originally entered politics as tools of native Americans. Many persons also feared that the immigrants would try to involve the nation in Europe's affairs as, for example, Ireland's quarrel with England and the German liberals' attempt to overthrow despotic rule in their homeland.

The European observance of Sunday, with its emphasis on pleasure and social life, was frowned on as contrary to the Puritan view of the Sabbath. The immigrants were accused of hurting the economy by taking jobs away from native Americans, and because among them were a good number who were unable to support themselves. Many immigrants were thought to be criminals and statistics were cited, such as the fact that in 1850 more than half the persons convicted of crimes were of foreign origin, although such people made up only about eleven percent of the population.

Organizations to support nativist policies arose in the 1840's. The Order of United Americans, for instance, was formed in 1844 and by 1855 had chapters in sixteen states and claimed 50,000 members. Through the Know Nothing movement, followed by the formation of the American party, nativism became a force to be reckoned with in several states between 1850 and 1855. In the latter year the movement reached its peak in political power, electing six governors as well as many legislators in a number of states, mostly in the East. Nativism's growth in power at this time was made possible, in part, because the Compromise of 1850 temporarily turned people's attention away from the North-South struggle over slavery. As that controversy heated up again, however, it overshadowed the nativist cause and divided its adherents on even more emotional issues— slavery and secession.

# 12  Industry and Labor

ALTHOUGH AGRICULTURE was the largest single factor in the economic life of the nation, the United States in 1850 was becoming increasingly industrialized. The Civil War speeded up the rate of this process, and was followed by an era of inventions and new techniques that further quickened the pace. In war and peace, labor, however, found it difficult to adjust to this growth and to organize effectively.

During the 1850's, American industry increased its use of steam power and of machine tools, while the system of producing interchangeable parts was applied to such products as clocks, farm implements and sewing machines. Even the South, presumably intent only on growing cotton, nearly doubled its manufacturing in the decade. By 1860, 1,500,000 workers were employed in American industry. While McCormick's factory in Chicago turned out 4,131 reapers in a year, most manufacturing was done by small units: 186 different furnaces produced pig iron, and sewing machines were made by seventy-four companies in twelve states. In terms of value added by manufacturing, the leading industries in 1860 were, in order: cotton textiles; lumber; boots and shoes; flour and meal; and men's clothing.

At the start of the war there was a brief recession but it ended quickly in the North when the government began to purchase the materials needed to fight a war. Besides articles of purely military use, such as rifles and ammunition, the Union army needed uniforms and associated items, such as tents and knapsacks. The sewing machine made it possible to turn out cotton and woolen goods in the quantities needed, while newer machinery that sewed soles to uppers kept the army shod. Cotton was not in as short supply as might have been thought, because after mid-1862 a good deal of it became available from occupied parts of the South. Even so, the manufacture of woolen cloth received an extra stimulus, the amount produced during the war increasing from 85,000,000 to over 200,000,000 pounds a year. Heavy industry prospered similarly: the amount of coal mined increased from 15,500,000 tons in 1861 to 22,792,000 tons in 1865, while 1,136,000 tons of pig iron were produced in 1864 compared with 731,344 in 1862.

With the impetus of the war, the number of manufacturing establishments grew in the decade of the 1860's by nearly eight percent while the number of wage earners increased by more than half. The industrial and business boom went on after the war so that the total value of property in the North and West (although not all of it was in manufacturing) grew from $10,000,000,000 in 1860 to $25,000,000,000 in 1870.

Many people became rich during the war, some by cheating and profiteering, some simply because business was so good. A whole society of newly rich grew out of wartime industry, while others were lucky, or insiders or crooks in mining and railroading. The wage earner did not do so well. Wages increased by about sixty percent during the war, but prices, although difficult to measure because of the lack of sound statistics and the fluctuations in currency values, went up far more. One general index of prices shows an increase of seventy-nine percent from 1860 to 1865. Another compilation of the cost of sixty absolute necessities records an increase of 125 percent.

Iron production had been a fundamental industry for many years, but it prospered even more after the war when the Bessemer process made possible the economical production of steel, much more durable than iron, on a large scale. The Bessemer process was discovered independently in 1857 by Sir Henry Bessemer (1813-98), a British engineer and inventor, and William Kelly (1811-88), an American inventor. The principle involved is the oxidation of impurities in iron by blowing air through the molten iron. Bessemer steel was first produced in the United States in 1865 and at once began to replace iron for many uses, especially the rails trains run over. Only 2,277 tons of such rails were produced in 1867 but by 1875 the figure was 259,699 tons.

Among the ironmasters of the period were Peter Cooper (1791-83), of the older generation, and Andrew Carnegie (1835-1919), the leader of the younger generation. Cooper established an iron works in 1829 and in 1852 the plant produced the first structural iron beam able to carry the weight of a large building. In 1852 he founded Cooper Union, an institute for the working man, and in 1870 was awarded a medal for having rolled the first iron for fireproof buildings. Carnegie was born in Scotland and his first position of importance was as a superintendent for the Pennsylvania Railroad in 1859. Five years later he began to invest in iron manufacturing, then took an active hand in managing iron works when he saw the importance of steel in the growth of the nation. By 1875, he was merging other firms into his and was becoming the dominant figure in the business as well as one of the wealthiest men in the country.

The petroleum industry, destined to change the lives of people all over the world, began from nothing in this period. Until 1859, petroleum was simply an oily substance that seeped to the surface in certain places and often ruined brine wells from which salt was procured. It was said to have medicinal powers and was sometimes bottled and sold for this purpose, such as "Kier's Petroleum or Rock Oil, celebrated for its wonderful curative powers." In 1855 two men sent a sample of petroleum to

Professor Benjamin Silliman, Jr., at Yale University, and when he explained oil's chemical properties they engaged Edwin L. Drake (1819-80) in 1858 to drill a well near Titusville, Pennsylvania. Drake hired a local brine-well driller named "Uncle Billy" Smith, and on August 27, 1859, after going down sixty-nine feet, they struck oil, which flowed out of the first producing well in the United States at the rate of about twenty barrels a day.

Almost at once an oil rush reminiscent of the California gold rush began. Men scrambled for land in the Pennsylvania oil field on which to drill wells, while boom towns grew up over night and disappeared just as fast. Within three years of Drake's discovery, 128,000,000 gallons were produced. Oil was an important export product by 1865, with $16,000,000 worth sold abroad. In another ten years the United States was exporting 150,000,000 gallons. At first prices fluctuated wildly, depending on the amount produced and on the manipulations of those trying to control the new industry. Oil sold for $20 a barrel in 1859; for 52 cents in 1861; and for $8 in 1863. The chief value of oil at this time was for the kerosene that could be distilled from it. Gasoline was a waste product until the day of the gasoline engine. The cracking process, which by heating the oil under pressure produced a bigger proportion of light oils, began to be used in 1862. This gave more kerosene for use in lamps. Kerosene rapidly displaced whale-oil lamps and candles, and as far away as China lamps burned with American kerosene.

As in the early days of gold mining, the new oil industry was an affair of individuals, with thousands drilling wells and others operating small refineries. After a few years there were 1,100 different companies. Then people who saw the need for more efficiency and the possibility of greater profits entered the industry. The man who became chief among them was John D. Rockefeller (1839-1937), a pious, hard-working soul who, with a job as a bookkeeper in Cleveland at sixteen, had in four years become a partner in a produce business. After another four years, seeing the almost limitless possibilities in oil, he and some partners established a refinery. Twenty of the twenty-six refineries in Cleveland, then the refining center, were in their hands in 1872, and two years later they acquired units in other cities. They formed the Standard Oil Company in 1870 and were intent on controlling not only the refining end but also the transportation of the crude oil from well to refinery and oil products from refinery to market. Rockefeller and his partners, in 1872, organized the South Improvement Company, an unusual organization that made agreements with the railroads concerning oil shipping rates. By this arrangement, Standard Oil not only got a rebate on its freight charges but also a "drawback" on freight paid by other oil companies—that is, the railroads gave Standard some of the money they received from Standard's rivals. Even in a day of free and easy business ethics, this aroused so much opposition that the company's charter was canceled after three months. Standard, nevertheless, went on its way toward near-monopoly by its efficiency; by more mergers, some of which were forced; and by the ruthless methods it used to crush those who would not join Standard. Rockefeller himself became the wealthiest man in the nation.

The food processing industry also became big business, as new methods of preserving food were developed. Philip D. Armour (1832-1901), who began his business career selling provisions to gold rush miners, established a meat packing plant in Chicago in 1868. At the processing end, he made use of just about every part of each animal, while at the distribution end he set up a sales organization and a delivery system that placed his products in markets hundreds of miles away. Gustavus F. Swift (1839-1903) did much the same, also in Chicago, and pioneered in devising refrigerated freight cars that made it possible to ship dressed beef to the East. Commercial canning prospered, and its products were especially useful in keeping mining prospectors in isolated camps and Civil War soldiers from starving. Canned pork and beans was a staple of the Union army's diet, while Columbia River salmon from the far Northwest were available in cans after 1866.

Until the controversy over slavery overshadowed everything else, the tariff had been an abrasive issue between the North and the South. It was, in fact, primarily responsible for the nullification crisis of 1832. The South accused the North of insisting on high tariffs which would increase the cost of goods in that section while protecting northern industries from foreign competition. The Tariff Act of 1857, however, reduced rates to a maximum of twenty-four percent, which was the lowest rate since 1815. Then in the 1859-60 session of Congress, Justin S. Morrill (1810-1898), a member of the House from Vermont, introduced a bill which greatly increased rates. The Morrill Act did not pass Congress, though, until February 1861, when many southern members had withdrawn. The most important changes were increases in duties on iron and wool. The Republicans meant it as a bid to industrial and farming interests while the South saw it as another piece of evidence that the North was determined to run roughshod over it.

During the conflict, tariff rates were steadily increased to raise revenue needed to finance the war. The biggest boost came in 1864 and made rates about forty-seven percent. A further increase was enacted in 1867, but in 1872 the Republicans, fearing they would lose votes among the general populace, put through a ten percent reduction. Three years later, however, this cut was rescinded and a tariff system for the protection of American industries, not just for revenue, became permanent into the next century. Industrialists were happy, but farmers were beginning to doubt this was in their interest.

Labor organizations had existed since early in the century, but until the 1850's most were local and small. In 1852, though, the National Typographical Union was founded and was followed on a national scale by the stone cutters in 1853, the hat finishers in 1854 and the molders and the machinists in 1859. The Civil War spurred the labor movement to further action. The controversy over slavery focused in part on a comparison of the economic and social status of the slave with the northern industrial worker. Then, during the war, workers were rightly upset when wages did not keep pace with prices, while the sudden affluence of war profiteers emphasized the growing gulf between rich and poor. All these factors caused labor to give more thought to organizing in order to exert more power. As a result, ten more national unions were formed between 1863 and 1866, including the first of the railroad brotherhoods, and by 1870 there were thirty-two national trade unions.

Strikes as a weapon to secure labor's demands were not new, but they were rather infrequent in the 1850's. The leaders of a strike of construction workers on a South Carolina railroad in 1855 were sentenced to two months in jail and fined $5. They were seeking an increase in pay from $1 to $1.25 a day. The most serious prewar strike was that of the shoemakers in Natick and Lynn, Massachusetts, in February 1860. The strike spread through New England until as many as 20,000 were striking. For perhaps the first time police and militia were called out, although there was no violence, and a good deal of public support for the strikers was apparent. Within two weeks the employers began to give in, and while few would recognize the unions, they did grant the wage increases for which the strike had been called. As the Civil War went on and labor's position became worse, the frequency of strikes grew: bricklayers in Chicago; horsecar drivers in New York; and printers in St. Louis, for example. In some cases martial law was declared and troops used as strikebreakers. Lincoln's sympathies were with the workers and he only once supported government intervention. Before the war he said: "Thank God we have a system of labor where there can be a strike." In the course of the war total union membership grew to about 200,000.

The National Labor Union, holding its first convention in 1866, was an attempt to form a national federation of labor organizations. Its president from 1868 until his sudden death the next year was William H. Sylvis (1828-69), who had been head of the iron molders union. The National Labor Union was reformist-minded and the first plank in its platform was a demand for the eight-hour day as the measure of a legal day's work. It also urged currency and banking reform and the restriction of immigration, particularly of Chinese. Becoming the National Labor Reform party in 1872, it collapsed when its venture into presidential politics was a complete failure.

For a period, the most successful union was the organization of boot and shoemakers called the Knights of St. Crispin. Organized in Milwaukee in 1867, it protested the introduction of shoemaking machinery that brought in unskilled labor. Its strikes were successful for a time and with 327 lodges by 1871 and a membership of about 50,000, it was the largest union in the country. But the Knights of St. Crispin, as well as being threatened by unskilled labor, also got involved in politics, picked some dishonest officers, suffered like others in the Panic of 1873, and by 1878 disappeared. Many of the members joined the Knights of Labor. This organization, founded in 1869 under the leadership of Uriah Stephens (1821-82), a Philadelphia garmentmaker, was at first a secret organization. It was also organized on an industrial basis rather than restricting membership to those in one particular craft. It held its first national convention in 1875, and after 1878 it was by far the most important labor group in the country for some years.

Quite another kind of organization was the Molly Maguires, a secret Irish-American group in the anthracite coal fields of eastern Pennsylvania. Its members protested and struck against the intolerable working and living conditions with little success, since the police took their orders from the owners. The Maguires resorted to violence and killed a number of officers of the law. The owners, too, instigated some of the violence against the mines so they would have an excuse to crush the Maguires. The Pinkerton detective agency was hired to infiltrate the group, which it did. As a result, twenty-four Maguires were convicted in 1874, ten of them were hanged and the organization's power broken.

Although wages went up during the wartime boom and inflation, some typical wages of the early 1850's show the general conditions of the period. Male factory workers were paid from $5 to $6 a week, but women received $2 less. Such skilled workers as blacksmiths, machinists, masons and carpenters could command $12 a week or more. At the other extreme, women needle workers, laboring at home, might make 25 cents a day at the most. Editor Horace Greeley, in 1851, estimated that a family of five needed $10.37 a week as a minimum income. By 1860 the average work day was eleven hours and was going down, while the Federal government established an eight-hour day for its employees in 1868. Most women who worked were in domestic and personal service, but 354,000 females over ten years of age were employed in manufacturing in 1870. At the same time, 739,000 children between the ages of ten and fifteen were at work. Some laws were passed to protect children, and Massachusetts was one of the leaders with an 1867 law that said children under sixteen could not work more than sixty hours a week.

Besides the usual grievances over wages and working conditions, labor faced, or thought it faced, other problems during this period. For a while many workers feared emancipation would release large numbers of blacks to compete with northern labor for jobs and that this would lower wages. As the war neared its end, some feared an oversupply of labor when thousands of soldiers took off their uniforms. Neither of these factors turned out to be important. Large-scale immigration posed a clearer threat because immigrants were sometimes used deliberately as strikebreakers. Of different races and nationalities, the immigrant workers sometimes quarreled among themselves and they also threw up language barriers. American craft unions were reluctant to accept immigrants and blacks, especially the latter, as members.

After the war, labor enjoyed a period of comparatively good times because prices came down some while wages tended to stay at their wartime levels. The Panic of 1873 and the ensuing depression changed the picture, however. By early 1874 about a quarter of the work force in New York City was unemployed. Protest meetings were held in many cities and one in January 1874, in Tompkins Square in New York, resulted in injuries to many people when mounted police charged a large crowd without warning.

By 1875, industry, together with its owners and managers, seemed to have advanced more in the quarter-century than had labor, both in comparison with the lot of the working man and the status of union organization. Overall, the pace of industrialization, spurred by the war, had been remarkable.

# 13 Business and Finance

THE EXTRAORDINARY needs of the Federal government in financing the Civil War dominated the fields of money and banking during much of the time from 1850 to 1875. The story of business and finance is similar to that of industry in the period: expansion during and after the war, marked by the rise of the newly rich, whose fortunes were sometimes acquired in questionable ways. Along with this, there were innovations in business practices and two depressions.

The Federal government had never faced any problem of the magnitude of financing the war. In the four years of conflict, it spent more than the previous total cost of government. The necessary money came from taxes, from borrowing and from the issuance of paper money. Customs duties had always been the primary source of government revenue and the tariff was raised to bring in still more. Internal taxes were placed on many products and processes so that income came in from excise levies on raw materials, on the manufacturing process and on sales. The nation also had its first income tax from 1861 to 1872. At the start, the tax was three percent on incomes over $800, but this was increased until those with incomes over $5,000 paid ten percent. Before it was abolished, the income tax raised $347,000,000. Through the sale of various kinds of bonds, the government, by 1865, raised $2,621,000,000, more than it took in from taxes. The total public debt on September 1, 1865, stood at the then unheard of sum of $2,846,000,000.

Without the services of Jay Cooke (1821-1905), the Treasury might not have been able to dispose of so many dollars' worth of bonds. Cooke founded a banking house in 1861 and during the war became the government's agent. He pioneered in advertising campaigns to sell war bonds in small denominations to individuals, and at one time had 1,500 agents at work. His commissions ran to $3,000,000 a year, but he had very large promotion expenses.

One aspect of war financing that caused controversy until the mid-seventies was the issuance of "greenbacks" under the Legal Tender Act of 1862. Greenbacks, so-called because of the green ink used in printing the backs of the notes, were issued on the credit of the United States. In effect, they were paper currency with no gold or silver behind them. The first issue totaled $150,000,000, and by September 1865, $433,160,000 in government notes were outstanding. Greenbacks were legal tender for paying public and private debts, but not for tariff duties, and they were not redeemable in specie. Beginning in 1866, the Treasury gradually reduced the greenbacks outstanding so that by 1868 the total in circulation was down to about $356,000,000. Farmers and other debtors objected to this reduction, wanting inflation in the form of cheaper money to pay off mortgages and other debts they had contracted when prices were high. The greenbacks were also factors in a debate over payment of the interest and principal on government bonds. Bonds had been bought with depreciated greenbacks during the war, so some people argued that the government should pay back the holders in the same way. The Republicans, however, who represented the interests of the banks and larger investors, believed all government obligations should be paid in gold, which was more valuable, and Congress passed a law to that effect in March 1869.

The controversy over the greenbacks also resulted in a

number of lawsuits that reached the Supreme Court, the first important one being decided in 1870. The Court, including Chief Justice Chase, who had been secretary of the treasury at the time the Legal Tender Act was passed, held the law unconstitutional, at least so far as it concerned payments on contracts or debts made before the law was passed. With the membership of the Court changed somewhat, the justices in a case the following year reversed the decision and said the greenbacks were completely legal. The fate of the greenbacks was finally settled by the Resumption Act of 1875, which provided that after January 1, 1879, the greenbacks would be redeemed in specie and that the quantity in circulation would be reduced to $300,000,000.

The United States had never had an adequate national banking system, but the war indirectly brought into being one that was more satisfactory. Banking was conducted mostly through banks chartered by states, of which there were 824 in 1850. Ten years later there were nearly 1,600 banks and 7,000 different kinds of bank notes in circulation, at least half of which were counterfeit or of no value. The National Bank Act of 1863, which was amended the next year, set up a new system. To qualify under its terms, a bank had to have one-third of its capital invested in United States securities, which helped the government sell its war bonds. Such banks could then receive from the government bank notes up to ninety percent of the market value of the bonds, and the notes were legal tender. Banks were slow to take advantage of these terms until, beginning in 1865, the government put a tax of ten percent on notes issued by state banks. This drove the state banks' notes out of circulation. Over 1,500 banks were in the new system by October 1865.

During the quarter-century, and after the war in particular, much private financing was needed in addition to what the government required. Very large sums of capital had to be raised to expand industry and, most of all, to build the trans-

Mississippi railroads. A few people and financial institutions as a result became very powerful in the economic life of the country. Among them was August Belmont (1816-90), who was German-born and emigrated to the United States in 1837. He represented the wealthy Rothschild interests of Europe and later founded his own bank. A strong pro-Union Democrat, Belmont's international position enabled him to exert influence on merchants and financiers in England and France that helped prevent recognition of the Confederacy. George F. Baker (1840-1931) was a founder of the National City Bank of New York in 1863 and later helped finance the Northern Pacific Railroad. J. Pierpont Morgan (1837-1913) grew to be the most powerful of all after he entered banking in New York in 1857. As early as 1869 he became involved in railroad financing and thereafter concerned himself chiefly with the roads, both in securing control of and merging those already built, and in financing new roads in the West.

Others in the world of finance were speculators at best, criminals at worst, although some were colorful characters. One was Daniel Drew (1797-1879), who began life as a cattle driver and always retained a rustic look. He was a devout Methodist and helped found Drew Theological Seminary. Drew forced his way onto the board of directors of the Erie Railroad in 1857. Among his associates was James Fisk (1834-72), who worked for a circus as a boy and who made a great deal of money during the war by buying up cotton in the South and by selling Confederate bonds in Great Britain. He established a brokerage house in 1866 and six years later was killed by a former associate in a quarrel over the favors of a well-known actress, Josie Mansfield. Fisk and Drew became associated with Jay Gould (1836-92), who started his business career as a store clerk.

Between 1866 and 1868, this trio was involved in a battle for control of the Erie Railroad with Cornelius Vanderbilt (1794-1877), who had first made a fortune in shipping. During the

Civil War Vanderbilt became interested in railroads and now wanted to secure control of the Erie, which, as a result of wartime business, was in very good financial condition. The unscrupulous trio outwitted Vanderbilt, partly by issuing unauthorized stock. Fisk and Gould then turned on Drew and ousted him. With Gould in control from 1868 to 1872 the Erie was financially wrecked to such an extent that it went into bankruptcy in 1878. Gould, in the course of his career, controlled the Western Union Telegraph Company and the New York City elevated railways, among other enterprises.

Gould and Fisk were also responsible for "Black Friday," September 24, 1869. Using the fact that the value of greenbacks fluctuated in terms of gold, the pair tried to organize a "corner" in gold. To succeed they had to keep the government from putting United States Treasury gold on the market, and in this connection they induced a brother-in-law of President Grant's to use his influence with the general. They did not hesitate to spread word that Grant was against selling government gold. The general was naïve but not dishonest, and when matters got to this point he ordered $4,000,000 of gold put on the market. The price of gold dropped sharply, ending the "corner" and ruining a number of speculators.

Growth and innovation in merchandising and retailing also marked the period. Mail-order selling, the chain store system and the modern department store had their origins in this quarter-century. In Chicago, Aaron Montgomery Ward, after working as a store clerk and a traveling salesman, saw a chance to sell goods directly to people in rural areas through catalogs sent them in the mail. He began his operation, which became Montgomery Ward and Company, in a modest way in 1872 with a one-sheet leaflet offering bargains to Grangers. George F. Gilman established what became the Great Atlantic and Pacific Tea Company in 1859, and by 1870 had eleven stores selling merchandise that carried his company's label.

Stores offering a variety of merchandise—the general store —were common in rural America, but in the cities most stores specialized in one or a few lines. The R. H. Macy store in New York began in 1858 as a general dry goods store, and in ten years was much like a modern department store. Meanwhile, though, the most important pioneer of department store operations was getting his start. He was Alexander T. Stewart (1803-76), who came to New York from Ireland about 1820. Three years later he was selling Irish laces, and in 1846 he opened a wholesale and retail dry goods store that by 1850 was the largest in the city. When he opened a newer store in 1862 it was the largest retail establishment in the world and set the pattern for everyone else. Stewart had 2,000 employees, whom he drove hard, but he was also a generous philanthropist. Stewart was one of the wealthiest men of his day, and his Fifth Avenue mansion was one of the sights of New York.

Marshall Field (1834-1906), who as a young man in 1856 left Massachusetts to settle in Chicago, began a career in merchandising that resulted in his partnership in 1865 in what became that city's first department store. Field was a pioneer in arranging large-scale purchases so as to be able to offer low prices, and he had buying agents around the world. John Wanamaker (1838-1922) worked his way up from errand boy to owner of a men's clothing business in Philadelphia in 1861. He opened a larger store in 1875, selling dry goods and clothing at first, that developed into one of the foremost department stores. Wanamaker established a one-price system and guaranteed customers their money back if they were dissatisfied.

Various types of insurance had been available for a long time, but life insurance was reformed and given a new impetus in the 1850's by "the father of life insurance," Elizur Wright (1804-85). Wright was a mathematician by training and an ardent and active abolitionist for many years. Interested in reform in general, he took up the cause of improving the business practices of life insurance companies. In 1853, with the aid of his children who did many of the necessary calculations, Wright brought out tables showing the reserve funds needed for 268 different kinds of insurance policies. Through his efforts, Massachusetts enacted a law in 1858 that required insurance companies to maintain proper reserve funds. Life insurance in force in 1860 amounted to $150,000,000; by 1870 the figure had climbed to $2,000,000,000.

Foreign trade was important in the economy of the nation, as it had been since colonial times. In spite of the war and the loss of shipping under the American flag caused by it, America's exports and imports grew. Except for 1862, imports exceeded exports through 1873. Beginning in 1874 and continuing to the end of the century, exports almost always were greater than imports. Exports in 1850 were $144,376,000 and imports $172,510,000; for 1860 the figures were $333,576,000 and $353,616,000.

The nation's economy was struck by two depressions in the quarter-century, the Panic of 1857 and the Panic of 1873. A variety of causes brought the first to a head. The end of the Crimean War cut down the European demand for American farm products and also affected shipbuilding and shipping. About the same time, a boom in western land speculation collapsed when it got out of hand. During the same period, the railroad system had been over-built in terms of what could be expected from such investments in the near future, while in the background was a generally weak banking system. The panic was triggered by the failure of an Ohio bank with a branch in New York. A run on New York banks by depositors wanting to withdraw specie followed, and it was of such an extent that by October 14 almost all banks in the country had to suspend specie payments. This depression was primarily financial, and recovery came fairly soon, but not before there was serious unemployment in the East in 1858 and some angry demonstrations by those out of work. The unemployed had to depend mostly on private charity, but a few municipalities created jobs on public works for them.

The Panic of 1873, although caused by many of the same reasons as the earlier depression, was more serious and lasted longer. Again, the end of a war in Europe—this time the Franco-Prussian War—reduced the demand for farm products. Mostly, though, the trouble stemmed from over-expansion in building railroads and unwarranted speculation in other fields. Now, too, the shoddy business ethics of the time showed up as stocks and bonds lost their value because far too many had been issued in relation to sound assets and business prospects. Over half the railroads defaulted on their bonds. The big crash came on September 17, 1873, when Jay Cooke's banking house failed. This brought down a number of other banks and caused the New York Stock Exchange to close for ten days. The depression became worldwide, with heavy unemployment in American cities. According to one report, 900 people starved to death in New York in 1873. Prosperity did not fully return for several years.

It was a unique quarter-century for American industry, business and finance. In a nation torn first by the slavery controversy and secession, and then by war on a scale never before seen on the continent, the Union's economic system successfully met the challenge of providing the materials and the money necessary to wage the war. Partly because of the war and partly because of other factors having to do with industrialization and technology, the economic system went on to expand even more after 1865. Somewhere in the process, though, the results of war profiteering began to appear. Business practices were less honest, corruption was evident both in business and government and, as the period ended, big industry and big business were in the saddle, dominating a subservient government as well as disregarding the worker and the consumer.

For the first time, serious and widespread criticism appeared and the intellectuals began to decry the triumph of unregulated business enterprise. Many people lost respect for the leaders of industry because of the type of men now in control. The younger Charles Francis Adams, son of the ambassador to Great Britain, economist and historian, brigadier general in the war and a railroad management expert who exposed the corrupt financing of the Erie Railroad, wrote later

> I have known and known tolerably well, a good many "successful" men—"big" financially—men famous during the last half-century; and a less interesting crowd I do not care to encounter. Not one that I have ever known would I care to meet again, either in this world or the next; nor is one of them associated in my mind with the ideas of humor, thought or refinement.

# 14 Transportation, Communication and Technology

BETWEEN 1850 and 1875 the railroad and the telegraph systems developed, both in scope and in importance, and clearly dominated transportation and communication. They also provided the technical and mechanical highlights of the era with the completion of the first transcontinental railroad and the laying of the first trans-Atlantic cable. American inventors, at the same time, were devising many new items for both industry and the home.

Railroads entered a period of rapid expansion around 1850, at which time there were almost 9,000 miles of track in the country. This increased to a little more than 30,000 miles in 1860. Even the start of the Civil War did not halt construction, although almost all of the 4,500 miles of track laid between then and 1865 were in the mid-Atlantic states and the Old Northwest. Another five years saw mileage continue to grow to almost 53,000 miles.

Most railroad companies operated only a few miles of track and the process of merging them financially and connecting them physically into longer routes was just beginning. An exception was the Erie Railroad, completed in 1851, between Piermont, near New York City, and Dunkirk, on Lake Erie, a distance of 483 miles, which made it the longest railroad in the world. When it opened, a special train carried many dignitaries, including President Fillmore and Daniel Webster, who rode in a rocking chair fastened to a flat car so he would not miss any of the scenery. The Pennsylvania Railroad connected Philadelphia and Pittsburgh in 1852. The next year, rail service between New York and Chicago was available, although not in one continuous line. St. Louis could be reached by train from Baltimore in 1857. The New York Central Railroad came into being in 1853, when seven short lines between Albany and Buffalo, New York, were combined into one.

The Pennsylvania and the New York Central expanded into two of the largest railroads in the East and the Midwest as a result of the leadership of Thomas A. Scott (1823-81) and Cornelius Vanderbilt, the first a railroad operator, the other a financier and speculator. Scott was general superintendent of the Pennsylvania in 1858 and for a time during the war was in charge of all government railroad transportation. As president of the line from 1874 to 1880, he expanded it greatly. Vanderbilt, although he lost his battle to get control of the Erie, was head of the New York Central by 1867, when the line ran from New York to Buffalo. By 1873, it went all the way to Chicago. Vanderbilt voted himself large quantities of stock and issued more stock than the road's assets justified, but he did greatly improve its equipment and service, cutting the running time between New York and Chicago from fifty to twenty-four hours.

In the Midwest, upon its completion in 1856, the Illinois Central Railroad, with 700 miles of main line tracks, became the longest railroad in the world. It was also the first to which the Federal government granted large amounts of public land as a subsidy. The Illinois Central received 3,736,000 acres. The impact of railroad building is indicated by the population growth along this line: in 1850 before it was built there were only ten towns on the route; by 1870 there were eighty-one towns and total population was up from 12,000 to 172,000.

The railroad network spread beyond the Mississippi, although there were only 3,000 miles of track in 1865. In five years, another 9,000 miles were added, and by 1880 the total was 32,000 miles of track. The trans-Mississippi lines were aided by lavish grants of public lands. The Atchison, Topeka and Santa Fe was given 3,000,000 acres in 1863. This was the line that eight years later reached Dodge City and helped make it the famous cowtown of legend. The Northern Pacific, which proposed building from Lake Superior to a Pacific coast port in the Far Northwest, received an even larger grant: 40,000,000 acres. It was nine years before the first 500 miles were completed. Congress made its last land grant to railroads in 1871 and by that time the total had reached 170,000,000 acres, given to more than eighty roads. About 35,000,000 acres of this were never turned over to the roads, but one expert estimates that the land the railroads did acquire title to was worth half a billion dollars.

The war brought prosperity to the northern railroads because of the great volume of freight and passengers they carried for the government. It was the first time the roads had made substantial profits, so much money before having gone into further construction. The Civil War was also the first war in which railroads played an important military role. Before its railroads were badly worn and damaged, the South was able to reinforce General Bragg at Chickamauga in 1863 by sending one of General Longstreet's corps of between 12,000 and 15,000 men from Richmond to northern Georgia. The movement was 900 miles over ten different railroads. A little later, the Union's greatest single troop movement took place when 25,000 men, ten batteries of artillery and all the accompanying horses were transported 1,200 miles from Washington to Tennessee in eleven and a half days to reinforce General Rosecrans in Chattanooga. The move required thirty trains of nearly 600 cars.

The engineer who kept the military railroads operating was Herman Haupt (1817-1905), who was a West Point graduate and later chief engineer of the Pennsylvania line. As head of construction and operation of military roads, he became known for the temporary bridges he was able to erect in record time. President Lincoln said of one that it seemed to be built "out of beanpoles and cornstalks." Haupt was also the engineer responsible for the Hoosac Tunnel in Massachusetts. Begun in 1856 and not finished until 1875, it was the first important railroad tunnel in the United States.

The dream of a railroad across the continent took form almost as soon as tracks began to spread over the nation, and the idea was given a strong impetus by the Mexican War, which made the United States a truly transcontinental nation. Controversy between the North and the South over what route the line should follow delayed the scheme. When the South was no longer represented in the Federal government, the problem disappeared and on July 1, 1862, with the war far from won, a bill was passed and signed that gave the signal to go ahead.

The legislation authorized the Union Pacific Railroad to build westward from Omaha, Nebraska, on the Missouri River, and for the Central Pacific Railroad to build eastward from Sacramento, California. Each company was to receive ten alternate sections (a section was 160 acres) of public land for each mile of track it built. Each line was also loaned $16,000 to $48,000 per mile from government funds, the amount depending on the difficulty of the terrain. Two years later, the government doubled the amount of land to be given. In California, ground was broken early in 1863 and in Omaha late that year, but not much construction actually took place until the war ended in 1865.

Track building became a race between the two companies, since the amount of public land and government loans they received depended on the number of miles of track each built. The Union Pacific had much easier land to build on—the prairies of Nebraska and the high plains of Wyoming, while the Central Pacific had to find a way to build a railroad through the Sierras, a steep mountain chain. The Union Pacific had as many as 10,000 men and about the same number of animals at work at the peak. Most of the workers were either ex-soldiers or ex-convicts from the East, or Irish immigrants from New York. Some of their time had to be spent fighting off Indians. In making haste, which the public wanted, much of the construction was not up to proper standards.

With a smaller population to draw on and much harsher working and living conditions, the Central Pacific had a hard time filling its construction crews until it hired about 6,000 Chinese laborers to add to 3,000 Irish. Some of the Chinese were brought from China just to work on the railroad. Toward the end of the race between the two companies, the Central Pacific laid ten miles of track in one day. By that time, in early 1869, both roads were laying track in Utah and had passed each other on parallel lines. Congress finally had to intervene and settle where the official junction would be. The spot chosen was Promontory Point, near Great Salt Lake. There, on May 10, 1869, trains from the two lines met, cowcatcher to cowcatcher, and a golden spike was driven into a crosstie to symbolize the link that now bound the nation together from the Atlantic to the Pacific. In all, the Union Pacific built 1,038 miles of track and the Central Pacific, 742.

Four men who were well on their way to dominating the economic and political life of California organized the Central Pacific, got it built and made fortunes in the process. Leland Stanford (1824-93), who went to California from New York State in 1852, became a successful merchant and an organizer of the Republican party in the West. He was governor of California from 1861 to 1863 and later a senator. Stanford handled the financial and political matters in which the "big four" got involved. Mark Hopkins (1813-78) and Collis P. Huntington (1821-1900), both from the East, became partners in a profitable hardware store after they joined the gold rush. Huntington was probably the most ruthless of the four, and his lobbying in Congress and bribery of the state legislature eventually gave him practical control of transportation in California and other parts of the West. The final member of the effective quartet was Charles Crocker (1822-88) who, like the others, had come West with the gold rush and had gone into business. He took charge of the actual construction, and it was he who brought in the Chinese laborers. The "big four" made extra and illicit profit for themselves out of the construction contracts, but unlike the Union Pacific and its Credit Mobilier, they did not get involved with Congress and consequently no public scandal erupted. In 1874, the Union Pacific fell under the control of Jay Gould, who looted it of $10,000,000 in ten years.

As trains carried people longer distances and as the public began to show a willingness to pay extra for luxuries, a demand arose for better dining and sleeping facilities. This demand was met by George M. Pullman (1831-97), a cabinetmaker who went to Chicago in 1858 and began converting ordinary railroad cars into units more suitable for long-distance travel. Pullman produced the first modern sleeping car in 1864, the "Pioneer," which made up part of the funeral train that carried Lincoln's body home to Springfield, Illinois, from Washington. Pullman founded the Pullman Palace Sleeping Car Company in 1867, and the next year introduced the first dining car designed as such. The demand for Pullman accommodations was large and the inventor grew rich.

The pioneers who settled the western prairies and the Great Plains would have found life almost impossible without the railroads, and the roads, in turn, could not have survived financially without the settlers. The rails stimulated settlement, and often the settlers came after a rail line was in existence. The railroads found it to their advantage to take an active hand in promoting settlement, not just from the East but also from Europe. They sent agents abroad and distributed enticing literature, printed in various languages. Other agents met immigrants at the eastern ports and some railroads built reception houses out west in which immigrants could stay while they looked around and chose land from the railroad's holdings. Liberal terms were offered; the Union Pacific in 1870 asked twenty-five percent down and the rest in three annual payments.

The ever-spreading railroad system created a demand for many bridges, and as trains grew heavier, bridges had to be stronger. At first, railroad bridges were built of wood, one of the most spectacular being that over the Genesee River at Portage, New York, built between 1851 and 1852. At its maximum height it was 234 feet above the ground and it took 1,500,000 board feet of lumber. It burned in 1875, as did most wooden railroad bridges eventually. Two engineers whose work greatly advanced bridge building were John A. Roebling (1806-69) and James B. Eads (1820-87).

Roebling was born in Germany, where he studied engineering, and came to the United States in 1831. He demonstrated that steel cable was of practical use and opened a plant to make it. Roebling was a pioneer in building suspension bridges, such as the one at Pittsburgh which he completed in 1846. His bridge over the Niagara River, completed in 1855, had an upper-level single-track rail line and a road for vehicles beneath it. In this bridge Roebling made the first large-scale use of his wire cable which was made of parallel wires that were wire-bound rather than of twisted wires. Another large bridge, over the Ohio River at Cincinnati, was built between 1856 and 1867. Roebling proposed a bridge over the East River in New York in 1857, but it was 1869 before his plans were approved and he was made chief engineer. Work had barely begun when Roebling was injured and died a few days later of tetanus. Work on what became the Brooklyn Bridge, not completed until 1883, was taken over by his son, Washington Roebling (1837-1926), who was also an engineer.

Eads, who invented a diving bell, and who, during the war, built a small fleet of ironclads that helped open the Mississippi for the Union, became internationally famous after he designed and built the Eads Bridge over the Mississippi River at St. Louis between 1867 and 1874. The bridge consists of three arches of steel, each more than 500 feet long, resting on masonry piers. A double-deck structure for use by both trains and road vehicles, the Eads bridge marked the first use of steel in a rigid structure.

Vertical transportation needed improvement at this time because buildings were being built higher. The problem was solved by Elisha G. Otis (1811-61), a Vermont-born inventor. In 1852 he perfected a device to keep hoisting machinery from falling, and from this he developed a safe passenger elevator. The first of its kind was installed in the Haughwout Department store in New York City in 1857.

Just as the railroads spread a transportation network over the land, telegraph wires wove a communication web from coast to coast. The nation east of the Mississippi was already well served by 1850 by Samuel F. B. Morse's invention of 1844. Congress voted to build a telegraph line from Missouri to California in 1860, and on October 24, 1861, the first message flashed over the wires. Ezra Cornell (1807-74), who had worked his way up from laborer to financier and who had supported Morse's experiments, founded the Western Union Telegraph Company in 1855. The last important rivals of Western Union, the American Telegraph Company and the United States Telegraph Company, were acquired by it in 1866, giving Western Union control of 75,000 miles of telegraph lines and creating a truly national service. The telegraph was essential to the railroads, since it was the only way messages could be sent ahead of trains to give operational orders. The Civil War provided the first major test of the value of telegraphy in military operations, and during the war some 6,000,000 messages were transmitted.

Thomas A. Edison (1847-1931), whose work on into the twentieth century made him America's most prolific inventor, began that career by improving the telegraph. Edison was first a newsboy on trains, but by the time he was sixteen he was a telegraph operator. Between 1870 and 1875 he devised a transmitter and receiver for an automatic telegraph, a system for sending four messages at once, and an improved stock ticker that printed 285 characters a minute.

After many efforts over nearly a decade, Europe and America were connected by a telegraph cable under the Atlantic. The promoter who refused to abandon the scheme when failure seemed certain was Cyrus W. Field (1819-92), a well-to-do merchant who first got the idea from a Canadian engineer in 1854. Field raised $1,500,000 from a group of New Yorkers and after five attempts between 1857 and 1858, a cable was completed between Ireland and Newfoundland on August 5, 1858. On the sixteenth, Queen Victoria and President Buchanan exchanged greetings, but after about three weeks the cable ceased working. No further attempt was made until 1865, when Field's organization tried again, using improved cable and techniques. The cable was lowered into the ocean from the steamship *Great Eastern*, which was five times bigger than any other ship then afloat. Once more the attempt failed, but a year later, in July 1866, the still undaunted Field saw success achieved with a permanently functioning cable.

The United States began to take a definite lead in industrial technology in the 1850's. The first milling machine, for cutting and shaping metals, was built in 1848. By the 1860's such equipment was in extensive use in America, but it was another decade before European manufacturers adopted it. Among other innovative machine tools was a turret lathe of 1855, used in gun factories, that contained eight different tools that could be applied separately and in turn for different parts of the manufacturing process. The sewing machine, originally thought of as a useful machine for the home, was adapted to industry. By 1860, 111,000 sewing machines a year were produced and many were in garment factories. At Troy, New York, in 1858, 3,000 such machines were in use for making shirts and collars. Ready-made clothing went up in value from $40,000,000 in 1850 to $70,000,000 ten years later.

Building on earlier attempts in Europe and America, Christopher L. Sholes (1819-90), a Milwaukee, Wisconsin, newspaper editor, in 1868 devised a patentable typewriter which the Remington Arms Company improved and put on the market in 1874. The typewriter was a boon to business and it also contributed to a social revolution when businesses started to hire women to operate it. The machine provided a door into the business world and to economic independence for women.

Another prolific inventor beginning his career at this time was George Westinghouse (1846-1914), who served in both the Union army and navy during the war. His first important invention came in 1869, when he patented an air brake, a revolutionary development that made train travel safe at high speeds. John W. Hyatt (1837-1920) invented celluloid, the first important synthetic plastic, in 1870, and began to manufacture it in 1872. He had been looking for a substitute for ivory in the production of billiard balls. Hyatt also invented a filter to purify water chemically and a type of roller bearing. Richard J. Gatling (1818-1903) invented and manufactured agricultural equipment, but he is remembered for his rapid-firing Gatling gun. He demonstrated it successfully to the Union army in 1862 but the army did not accept it until 1866, when the war was over.

Inventions and technological improvements for the home and the individual appeared in increasing numbers. An ice box patented in 1858 was better than any available before, and a suction-type vacuum cleaner was invented in 1869. The wet collodion process, whereby a glass plate is sensitized just before use by dipping it in a silver nitrate solution, popularized photography by making it simpler.

Gail Borden (1801-74) as a young man joined one of the early colonies of United States citizens in Texas, and as a surveyor he laid out the city of Galveston. Returning to New York in 1851, he began work on a process for evaporating milk, and in 1856 received a patent. His first plant to produce condensed milk began operations in 1858. In a day when much milk was contaminated and adulterated, Borden's milk was soon recommended by physicians. It was also a great boon to the army during the war.

In spite of America's involvement in the slavery controversy and the war, this quarter-century was marked by important technological and industrial advances, especially in the maturation of the railroad and telegraph systems.

# 15 The Intellectual Life and Literature

THE CIVIL WAR marked a dividing point in American intellectual and literary life. Before the war, the gentle, lofty transcendentalism of New England in the North, and the romantic cavalier spirit in the South were the most noticeable aspects of thought and writing. After the war, the North turned its attention to the new industrial world and its major authors paid surprisingly little attention to the recent war. In the South, however, defeat and nostalgia for a destroyed past were reflected in almost everything written.

Ralph Waldo Emerson (1803-82) established himself in the 1840's as the leading intellectual not only of New England but of the country. After 1850 he became a strong, almost violent, abolitionist but continued to deliver his popular lectures which advocated self-reliance, the spiritual nature of reality and the obligation to be optimistic, in keeping with transcendental thought. Emerson's lectures were issued in book form, such as *Representative Men* in 1850 and *The Conduct of Life* in 1860. Among those who followed in Emerson's intellectual footsteps was Henry David Thoreau (1817-62), also of Concord, Massachusetts. Thoreau, though, did not participate in the affairs of the world as Emerson did. Between July 1845 and September 1847, he lived alone in a cabin he built at Walden Pond, supplying his own needs. Out of this experience came his classic, *Walden* (1845), an account of his solitary life there.

The Civil War period also saw the start of the worldwide intellectual, scientific and theological revolution caused by the theory of evolution as expounded by Charles Darwin (1809-82), the English naturalist, in *Origin of Species* (1859) and *The Descent of Man* (1871). Darwin's theory that each species had not been separately and specially created, but that all were the result of natural evolution began a controversy in scientific and theological circles that was far from settled by 1875. Most scientists, however, were inclined to accept the new doctrine, while growing numbers of clergymen found ways of reconciling Christianity and evolution. John Fiske (1841-1901), a Connecticut-born scholar, became the chief popularizer of the new scientific concepts, beginning with *The Outlines of Cosmic Philosophy* in 1874.

Three writers who dominated American literature into the twentieth century first had works published in the 1860's. They were Mark Twain (Samuel Langhorne Clemens, 1835-1910), William Dean Howells (1837-1920) and Henry James (1842-1910). Although of military age, none served in the war and none made any important use of the war in his writings. Twain, born in Missouri, first learned the printer's trade, but in 1857 became a Mississippi steamboat pilot. Going west to Nevada in 1862, Twain got a job as a newspaper reporter and started writing humor in the frontier tradition. His story about a jumping frog won him recognition in 1865. Twain's travel writings, as in *The Innocents Abroad* (1869) and *Roughing It* (1872), brought him more readers. The satirical novel, *The Gilded Age* (1873), on which he collaborated with Charles Dudley Warner, gave a name to the period. Twain, in 1875, was well on his way to lasting popularity and literary esteem.

Howells was born in Ohio and like Twain learned the printing trade while young. He wrote a campaign biography of Lincoln in 1860 and was rewarded with an appointment as

American consul in Venice, which resulted in *Venetian Life* (1866). Back in the United States, Howells was taken up by the New England intellectuals and in 1871 became editor of the *Atlantic Monthly*, the most prestigious magazine of its day. His first novel, *Their Wedding Journey*, appeared in 1872, but his best work as a novelist and an early realist came after 1875. James wrote essays for the *Atlantic* in the 1860's and his earliest important fiction, a short story, appeared in 1871. His first novel was not published until 1876, by which time James was living in Europe, chiefly in London.

Nathaniel Hawthorne (1804-64) had been published as far back as the late 1820's, but his two best known works, *The Scarlet Letter* and *The House of the Seven Gables*, appeared in 1850 and 1851 respectively. He wrote a campaign biography of his friend Franklin Pierce, which secured him an appointment as consul at Liverpool from 1853 to 1857. Later he wrote *The Marble Faun* (1860). Almost all his writings describe in fictional form Puritanism and its decay. Herman Melville (1819-91) won many readers with his first five books, the last of which was *White-Jacket* (1850), but the book later generations deem his masterpiece, *Moby-Dick* (1851), was poorly received. The symbolism confused readers and they were even more baffled by *Pierre* the following year. Melville gradually gave up trying to support himself by writing and died after years of obscurity. Oliver Wendell Holmes (1809-99) had a double career as an eminent physician and as a poet and essayist. Some of his magazine pieces were collected in *The Autocrat of the Breakfast Table* (1858) and similar collections followed in 1860 and 1872. *Elsie Venner* (1861) was the first of three books he called "medicated" novels—all studies in abnormal psychology.

Among younger writers, Bret Harte (1836-1902) left New York for California and made his reputation writing about the mining frontier, while Edward Eggleston (1837-1902) left Indiana for New York but wrote mostly about the Middle West he knew. Harte was a printer and journalist in San Francisco in 1860, but the local-color stories he wrote for the new *Overland Monthly*, beginning in 1868, brought him popularity when published in *The Luck of Roaring Camp and Other Sketches* in 1870. Harte returned to the East and wrote prolifically, but he seemed to have lost his touch and his popularity declined. Eggleston was a Methodist minister who, in 1874, founded a church in Brooklyn. He was already well-known for his novel *The Hoosier Schoolmaster* (1871). Like his other works, it was pious in tone but realistic in its description of frontier life. He wrote *The Circuit Rider* in 1874.

The book that had the greatest impact on the nation was an antislavery novel, *Uncle Tom's Cabin*, by Harriet Beecher Stowe (1811-96). Published in March 1852, it sold more than 300,000 copies in its first year, was denounced throughout the South and did much to increase abolitionist sentiment in the North. Mrs. Stowe was born in Connecticut and had a strong religious background through her father, Lyman Beecher, a clergyman who became the first president of Lane Seminary in Cincinnati. There Mrs. Stowe was exposed to fierce abolitionist sentiment, and in Kentucky she observed the slave system at first hand. It was, however, the Fugitive Slave Act of 1850 that apparently aroused her to write the novel. In 1856 she wrote another novel, *Dred*, about the effects of slavery on the whites. *Uncle Tom's Cabin* attracted so much attention that when Lincoln met Mrs. Stowe he is said to have remarked: "So you're the little woman who wrote the book that made this great war." Later, Mrs. Stowe wrote books with a New England background. She bought a southern plantation after the war to try to help the blacks but the project was an economic and sociological failure.

Already internationally recognized, Henry Wadsworth Longfellow (1807-82) was also the most popular poet in the country. He added to his reputation after 1850 with more successful works. Among them was *Hiawatha* (1855), of which his publishers put out 11,000 copies in the first month. *The Court-ship of Miles Standish* (1858) was equally successful. *Tales of a Wayside Inn*, which included "Paul Revere's Ride," was published in 1863. When Longfellow gave up his professorship at Harvard in 1855, he was succeeded by James Russell Lowell (1819-91), another New Englander who was also a poet and essayist. Lowell became the first editor of the *Atlantic* in 1857, and through his wife's influence became an abolitionist. Most of his writings after 1850 were of a scholarly nature, except for essays in the magazine which criticized Great Britain's stand during the war. John Greenleaf Whittier (1807-92), of Quaker background, was a published poet in his twenties, then turned his attention to the antislavery movement. During and after the war he went back to poetry, writing the narrative poem "Barbara Frietchie," and his most popular book, *Snow-Bound* (1866).

In 1855, the same year that Longfellow's successful *Hiawatha* was published, a New York poet, Walt Whitman (1819-92), issued his first book of verse, *Leaves of Grass*. It received little attention and he was unable to sell even the 1,000 copies he had paid to have printed. Whitman earlier had been a teacher and a newspaper editor, and during the war was a volunteer nurse in Washington. He issued a number of editions of *Leaves of Grass*, including new poems, and the 1860 edition cost him his government job as a clerk because the secretary of the interior thought it was immoral. His most important prose work was *Democratic Vistas* (1871), in which he expressed his views on democracy and individualism. Whitman was much taken with Lincoln, and his grief at Lincoln's assassination is revealed in "O Captain! My Captain!" Eventually Whitman was recognized as a major American poet, expressing the aspirations of democracy and individualism.

John Lothrop Motley (1814-77) and Francis Parkman (1823-93) in the East, together with Hubert Howe Bancroft (1832-1918) in the West, were the leading contributors to the field of history. Motley devoted his life to a historical study of the Netherlands, in part because he saw an analogy between the Dutch, with their struggle for Protestantism and freedom in northern Europe, and the birth and growth of the United States. His major work, *The Rise of the Dutch Republic*, appeared in 1856. Motley served with skill as ambassador to Austria and to Great Britain, but in both cases he was recalled because of political differences, first with President Johnson and then President Grant.

Boston-born Parkman went West and traveled across the prairies before 1850 in the hope of improving his poor health. The result was *The Oregon Trail* (1849), after which he turned to his *History of the Conspiracy of Pontiac* (1851), an account of the Indian uprising of 1763-66 against the British. His life was spent mostly, however, on a series of seven books dealing with the conflict between France and Great Britain in the New World. Parkman saw it as a struggle between Protestantism and democracy on the one hand, and Catholicism and military despotism on the other. The books appeared between 1865 and 1892, beginning with *Pioneers of France in the New World*. He wrote both good history and good literature.

Bancroft went west from Ohio in 1852 intending to be a miner, but instead he established the largest bookstore and publishing firm west of Chicago. He collected material on the history of the area, including the Indians, and his collection reached 60,000 or more items. With his assistants, whose names never appeared on the books, Bancroft produced more than fifty volumes, starting with five volumes of *History of the Native Races* (1874-75).

After the war a number of intellectuals and writers left the South for the more prosperous North where opportunities for careers seemed better. Those authors who remained in the South—and some who left—wrote mostly in defense of the region and the "lost cause." Prewar days were glorified and nostalgia was evoked regularly. Paul Hamilton Hayne (1830-86), for example, can be considered "the last literary cavalier." His health prevented him from serving in the Confederate army, but he wrote well-received martial lyrics. Before the war he had been known for his nature poetry. Impoverished by the war, he continued to write fragile verse, published as *Legends and Lyrics* in 1872. Another poet, Henry Timrod (1828-67), is usually called "the laureate of the Confederacy," and he, too, was ill and poor. Among his *Poems* (1873), which Hayne edited, is his "Ode" to the Confederate dead. Sidney Lanier (1842-81) served in the Confederate army and was a prisoner of war for four months. Like Hayne and Timrod, he found himself ill and poor when the war ended, and wrote a novel, *Tiger-Lilies* (1867), about his war experiences. He then turned to writing poetry.

John Esten Cooke (1830-86) of Virginia was in many ways typical of both prewar and postwar southern authors. Before the war he wrote romantic tales of colonial Virginia, such as *Henry St. John, Gentleman* (1859). After fighting on the Confederate side throughout the war, Cooke wrote a series of romances, including *Hilt to Hilt* (1869), in which he depicted the war as seen by an imaginary aide to General Stonewall Jackson. Cooke wrote entertainingly, but he also idealized the past. John W. DeForest (1826-1906) was born in Connecticut, but on the basis of his service in the South, first with the Union army and then with the Freedmen's Bureau, he was able to write novels that accurately depicted both the war and the southern point of view. In *Miss Ravenel's Conversion from Secession to Loyalty* (1867) he wrote the first realistic novel about the great conflict. *Kate Beaumont*, published in 1872, examined the life and customs of South Carolinians as DeForest had observed them.

American humor continued to be expressed mostly in rural or frontier dialect. Artemus Ward (Charles Farrar Browne, 1834-67) was born in Maine but began his humorous writings in 1858 for the Cleveland *Plain Dealer*. "Artemus Ward's Sayings" told of the adventures of an imaginary showman as though written by a Down East character, with comic misspellings. Josh Billings (Henry Wheeler Shaw, 1816-85) was also a New Englander and, after trying his hand at being a coal miner, a farmer, a real estate dealer and at other occupations, he began, at forty-five, to write humorous sketches. Like Ward's writings, Billings's were those of a "cracker barrel philosopher," with deliberate misspellings, puns and dislocated grammar. His work was first collected in *Josh Billings, His Sayings* in 1865, and from 1869 to 1880 he issued an annual *Farmer's Allminax*.

Petroleum V. Nasby (David Ross Locke, 1833-88) became famous during the war with letters first published in an Ohio newspaper. Nasby was presumably an illiterate country preacher who supported the South, but his foolish arguments made his cause seem ridiculous. Like Ward and Billings, Nasby depended on backwoods spelling and grammar, along with mixed up logic. Lincoln was fond of Nasby's writings and read the latest one to his cabinet just before outlining his plans for the Emancipation Proclamation. *The Nasby Papers* (1864) was the first collection in book form. Robert Henry Newell (1836-1901), a New York journalist, wrote under the name of Orpheus C. Kerr ("office seeker") and jibed at politics and the avid aspirants for office. Lincoln was fond of these writings, too, and they were collected in book form. Newell married the popular actress Ada Isaacs Menken. In the same manner that Locke's Nasby indirectly sided with the North, Bill Arp, the creation of Charles Henry Smith (1826-1903), was anti-Yankee by ineptly sympathizing with the North. Smith began these writings in 1861 in letters addressed to "Mr. Abe Linkhorn" which appeared in a Georgia newspaper. After the war Smith changed Arp into the typical shrewd philosopher of the cracker-barrel variety.

Those who wrote and edited for children included first-rate authors and popularizers. Mary Mapes Dodge (1831-1905), as editor of the wonderful magazine *St. Nicholas*, founded in 1873, was the most influential editor of the time in the field of children's literature. She was also the author of the very popular *Hans Brinker; or, The Silver Skates* (1865), among other writings. Louisa May Alcott (1832-88) was a daughter of Bronson Alcott, a somewhat impractical educator and reformer, and she grew up under the influence of Emerson and the transcendentalists. She helped support her family and served as a nurse in a Union hospital during the war until her health gave out. Her successes as an editor of writings for children began in 1867, and the next year she published *Little Women*, an account of her own and her sisters' early years. *Little Men* followed in 1871. She earned financial security for her family and participated in several reform movements.

William Taylor Adams (1822-97) and Horatio Alger (1834-99) were also successful authors of books for young people. Besides editing a magazine, Adams, under the name of Oliver Optic, wrote more than 1,000 short stories and 115 novels. He related exciting adventures, mixed with patriotism, while his heroes were always moral and even priggish. Alger, after graduating from the Harvard Divinity School and then revolting against such a background to lead a bohemian life in Paris, settled down in New York to write about 125 inspirational stories. They all told of poor boys who by hard work (or, sometimes, by luck) became successful, as in the Raggedy Dick series, which began in 1867.

Sentimental and moralistic tales for adult readers were equally popular. Among the most successful authors was Augusta Jane Evans (1835-1909) of Alabama, whose greatest success was *St. Elmo* (1867), the story of a dissipated young man who is reformed by the goodness of the heroine. This, and other works, brought the author more than $100,000. Josiah G. Holland (1819-81), the first editor of *Scribner's Monthly*, wrote both prose and poetry, always with a moral lesson. With a religious background set in seventeenth-century Connecticut, *The Bay-*

*Path* (1857) was one such novel while *Bitter-Sweet* (1858) was didactic poetry. It sold 90,000 copies.

Timothy Shay Arthur (1809-85) was the author of nearly 100 moral tales and tracts, the most popular of which was *Ten Nights in a Barroom and What I Saw There* (1854), which sold around 100,000 copies a year for some years, and when adapted for the stage played for fifty years. Edward Everett Hale (1822-1909), a Boston clergyman and philanthropist, was a prolific author best remembered for one short story which first appeared in the *Atlantic* in 1863: *The Man Without a Country*. The story, written out of patriotic motives during the war, was suggested by a remark of Vallandigham, the Copperhead, in which he implied that he did not care to live in a country that put up with Lincoln as president.

The war left many bereaved mothers, wives and sisters who turned to religious writings for solace. Among those who filled this need was Elizabeth Stuart Phelps Ward (1844-1911), whose mother also wrote religious fiction and whose emotional novel, *The Gates Ajar* (1868), was published under her maiden name. It is the story of a New England girl, overcome by the death of her brother in the war, who is slowly convinced by an aunt that there is indeed a life after death. The author asserted: "The angel said unto me 'Write!' and I wrote." The book sold 100,000 copies.

# 16 Art, Music, the Theater

THE WAR, quite naturally, interrupted careers and activities in every field, but in the quarter-century as a whole, art, music and the theater prospered. Although most artists and musicians studied abroad, and the country depended very much on European musicians and playwrights, there was an Americanizing trend in all fields, as well as one toward more professionalism.

Harvard University appointed Charles Eliot Norton (1827-1908) to the first chair of fine arts in America in 1874. And in the early 1870's the Boston Museum of Fine Arts, the Metropolitan Museum of Art in New York and the Corcoran Gallery of Art in Washington were all founded. The last was endowed by William W. Corcoran (1798-1888), a successful banker, who retired in 1854 to devote himself to art collecting and philanthropy.

The Hudson River School of painting dates from 1825 and it continued for half a century. Among older painters whose canvases reflected the school's interest in wild and untrammeled landscapes, and who found their subject matter in the Hudson River Valley, the Catskills and the White Mountains was Asher B. Durand (1796-1886). He painted portraits of several presidents as well as landscapes such as *In the Woods* and *Mountain Forest*. The early work of George Inness (1825-94) was in the Hudson River School tradition, but as time went on, his style became freer and he sought the mystical in nature. He is usually

considered the best American landscape painter of the nineteenth century and works such as *Peace and Plenty* brought him
popular acclaim. John Frederick Kensett (1818-72) produced
delicately colored landscapes that emanated a poetic feeling and
they earned him fame and a good deal of money. Frederick E.
Church (1826-1900), whose style was that of the school, preferred foreign scenery that enabled him to paint more exotic
landscapes.

Eastman Johnson (1824-1906), although he turned to por-
traiture in later life, was primarily a genre painter—scenes of
everyday life. His subject matter varied from *Corn Husking*
(1860) and *Nantucket Interior* (1865) to a large portrait, done in
1871, of a well-to-do New York family with fifteen people in the
painting and showing the heavy, ornate furniture of the time.
Emanuel Leutze (1816-68), born in Germany, painted historical
scenes that had more patriotic than esthetic value. Best known
are *Washington Crossing the Delaware* (1850) and an enormous
mural in the Capital in Washington entitled *Westward the Course
of Empire Takes Its Way* (1861). Albert Bierstadt (1830-1902) was
also born in Germany, and when he came to the United States he
joined a trail-making expedition in the Far West in 1859. Out of
his experience came the immense canvases that made him popular. They emphasize the grandeur and the drama of the region
in such paintings as *The Rocky Mountains* and *The Last of the
Buffalo*.

Three outstanding painters whose careers began at this
time were James Abbot McNeil Whistler (1834-1903), Winslow
Homer (1836-1910) and Thomas Eakins (1844-1916). Whistler
was dismissed from West Point (he did poorly in chemistry) in
1854, the next year went to Paris and in 1859 settled in London.
There he became known as a wit and a dandy as well as a painter
and etcher. His first success came in 1863 with *The Little Girl in
White*. He painted the picture popularly called *Whistler's Mother*
in 1872. Whistler was strongly influenced by Oriental art and

developed a delicate sense of color and design. Homer, beginning his career as a magazine illustrator, was sent to the battlefront by *Harper's Weekly* in 1861. The illustrations he drew on this assignment not only made him well known but also provided him with material for later paintings, such as *Prisoners from the Front* (1866). After 1875 he turned to watercolors and to seascapes. Eakins was far more realistic than the taste of his early days would accept, as in *The Gross Clinic* (1875), depicting a class in anatomical dissection, which caused a scandal. He was not allowed to show it at the Centennial Exhibition. Eakins also painted a number of rowing scenes, such as *The Biglen Brothers Racing* (1873).

Sculptors abounded and a considerable part of the work they did was of a patriotic nature, designed for public buildings and parks. Clark Mills (1810-83), although he had never seen Andrew Jackson or an equestrian statue, created, in 1853, the famous one in Lafayette Park in Washington which was the first equestrian-portrait statue done in America. With the horse rearing on its hind legs, the statue is more a mechanical marvel than anything else, but Congress was so enthusiastic it doubled Mills's commission. He did a very large equestrian statue of George Washington, which was dedicated in 1860. Thomas Crawford (1813-57) also sculpted the general on horseback in Richmond, Virginia, and *Armed Freedom* for the dome of the Capitol, which was cast in 1860 after his death. A better, more natural and less pretentious statue of Washington on horseback is that by Henry Kirke Brown (1814-86), which stands in Union Square in New York. He also sculpted four statues for the Capitol.

Unlike most American sculptors of the time, Erastus Dow Palmer (1817-1904) did not study in Italy. He was interested mostly in religious and American historical themes. His first full-length statue was *The Indian Girl*, and his most famous work is *The White Captive* (1859). William Wetmore Story (1818-95) was the son of a Supreme Court justice and wrote two legal treatises before turning to sculpture in 1847. His work consisted largely of figures of women in the classical style, such as *Cleopatra*, and rather stiff portraits of public figures. John Quincy Adams Ward (1830-1910) was apprenticed to Henry Kirke Brown and in his career turned out many strong sculptures of American heroes and events. Typical are *Indian Hunter* (1864) in Central Park in New York and a war memorial, *Private of the Seventh Regiment*. Harriet Goodhue Hosmer (1830-1908) lived mostly in Rome, where she produced graceful statues that very much suited the taste of the time. Thirty copies of her *Puck* (1860) were made.

The most popular sculptor was John Rogers (1829-1904), who created many small pieces, each portraying in a sentimental or humorous manner some scene of everyday life. His best known work was *The Slave Auction* (1859) because the abolitionists publicized it in support of their views. Other works treated such subjects as *Village Schoolmaster, Going to the Minister* and *The Wounded Scout*. About 100,000 reproductions of his works were sold in his lifetime at prices from $5 to $10.

Before the war a number of opera companies and orchestras, as well as individual performers, brought classical music to America. The Pellegrini Italian opera troupe, for example, toured the United States as far as San Francisco in 1853. Another, the Parodi company, opened a new theater in St. Louis. When war came, however, many European musicians went home, while others did not make the trips they otherwise might have. After the war more young Americans sought musical careers, and singing lessons were widely available, although professional training on instruments still required study in Europe. The start of self-sufficiency in music can be seen in the founding of the Oberlin Conservatory of Music in 1865 and the beginnings of the New England Conservatory, the Chicago Musical College and the Cincinnati Conservatory in 1867.

The leading conductors were all foreign-born and the most

active of them was Theodore Thomas (1835-1905), who came from Germany in 1845. When only sixteen, he went on tour as a violin soloist, but he spent most of his life conducting orchestras. He founded his own in 1862 and toured the United States with it every year from 1869 to 1878. Thomas introduced major works of Liszt, Wagner, Brahms and others to Americans. A French conductor, Louis Antoine Jullien (1812-60), who toured the United States with his orchestra in 1853-54, owed his success as much to showmanship as to musicianship. Conducting with a jeweled baton, Jullien included such numbers as the "Fireman's Galop," at the climax of which the ceiling of the orchestral hall was set afire—and was extinguished. He directed a Grand Musical Congress in 1854 with his baton raised over 1,500 instrumentalists and sixteen choral societies. Jullien was outdone in quantity, though, by Patrick S. Gilmore (1829-92), born in Dublin. He formed his own band in Boston in 1859, and when the war started the band enlisted as a unit. After the war he organized a number of spectacular music festivals, the biggest of which was the World Peace Jubilee in Boston in 1872, where he led a band of 2,000 and a chorus of 20,000. Leopold Damrosch (1832-85) came to New York from Germany in 1871 and in 1873 founded the Oratorio Society. He also founded the New York Symphony Society in 1878.

American composers were not plentiful, although George F. Bristow (1825-98) wrote one of the earliest operas by an American, *Rip Van Winkle*, in 1855. He also composed an "Arcadian Symphony" in 1874. Dudley Buck (1839-1909), an organist who was also an assistant orchestra conductor to Theodore Thomas, composed a good deal of church and other choral music. Among American performers was Louis Moreau Gottschalk (1829-69), born in New Orleans, who was a prodigy as a pianist, giving concerts at the age of twelve. He made his New York debut in 1853 and was acclaimed on tours of Europe and South America. Gottschalk also composed symphonic poems and piano pieces, such as "The Dying Poet," which was very popular in his day but did not survive. Adelina Patti (1843-1919) was born in Spain but was trained in the United States and became the most popular coloratura soprano of the time. She made her New York debut in 1859 and was applauded in London, Paris and Madrid as well.

John S. Dwight (1813-93) and William Henry Fry (1813-64) were the first two Americans to write music criticism of consequence. Dwight founded *Dwight's Journal of Music* in 1852 and edited it for twenty-six years. He never had more than 500 subscribers, but they were all influential in the field. Fry became music critic of the New York *Tribune* in 1852, the first such writer on an American paper. He was also the composer of what is regarded as the earliest American opera, *Leonora* (1845). He wrote a second one, *Notre Dame de Paris*, which was produced in Philadelphia in 1864. William Mason (1829-1908), son of the pioneer in music education, Lowell Mason, could have had a career as a concert pianist but turned mostly to teaching. After studying with Franz Liszt in Europe, he, with Theodore Thomas, formed a chamber music ensemble which for thirteen years helped arouse American interest in this kind of music. John Knowles Paine (1839-1906), a composer, organist and educator, began teaching music at Harvard in 1862 and in 1875 was appointed there to the first professorship of music in an American university. Many of his later pupils were prominent in the music field.

American Negro spirituals became widely known and appreciated in this period, beginning with the publication of *Negro Slave Songs of the United States* in 1867. They were enjoyed and appreciated much more after 1871, when the Fisk Jubilee Singers of Fisk University began giving concerts around the country and in Europe. The spirituals, which came out of the slave experience, combined African rhythms with the religious music of the Baptists and Methodists in the prewar South.

Although the Civil War caused some disruption in the theater, especially in the schedules of touring stock companies, it increased interest in such things as dramatizations of *Uncle Tom's Cabin*. Four different Uncle Tom shows played in New York at the same time. New York by mid-century was the theatrical center of the country, with six theaters plus several music halls. The spread of the railroads and urban growth also made it possible for more road companies to exist and to perform in more cities. Counting four in Brooklyn, New York had twenty theaters in 1868 and by the next year San Francisco had its own stock company.

The most prolific playwright of the time was Dion Boucicault (1822-90), who was born in England and came to the United States in 1853. He wrote or adapted about 150 plays. Among them was *The Octoroon; or, Life in Louisiana* (1859), which made him the first dramatist to treat the American black seriously. One of the most popular plays ever produced in America was Boucicault's stage version of Washington Irving's story *Rip Van Winkle* (1865). The star of the play was Joseph Jefferson (1829-1905), third of that name of a family of actors of English origin. Jefferson made the part so much his own that he played almost nothing else for the next fifteen years. Boucicault also wrote the first play based on the Civil War, *Belle Lamar* (1874). Less popular as a playwright was George Henry Boker (1823-90), who wrote in blank verse and used historical romance as his subject matter. One such play was *Leonor de Guzman* (1853). Bronson Howard (1842-1908) began as a newspaperman and became the first American dramatist to earn a full living from playwriting. His early success was a farce, *Saratoga*, in 1870.

The Drew family was prominent both in acting and in theater management. John Drew (1827-62), born in Ireland, made his New York debut in 1846, but was associated mostly with the Arch Street Theater in Philadelphia, which he managed. His wife, Louisa Lane Drew (1820-97), was on the English stage as a small child and played Lady Macbeth when she was sixteen. A very strong personality, she took over the management of the Arch Street Theater when her husband died. One of their children, a younger John Drew (1853-1927), acted at an early age in his mother's stock company and played his first important role in 1875 in New York. John E. Owens (1823-86), although born in London, became famous in the United States as an interpreter of Yankee stage characters. As a comedian whose facial expressions were a great asset, Owens's most famous role was as Solon Shingle in *The People's Lawyer*. Frank S. Chanfrau (1824-84) was a hit before 1850 as Mose, a New York fireman, in several plays that depended on fast action and the actor's personality. He was a hit again as a pioneer, Kit Redding, in *Kit the Arkansas Traveller*, w.hich he played from 1870 to 1882.

The tragic actor Edwin Booth (1833-93) was one of America's first truly great actors and the first to earn a reputation in Europe also. He set a record in 1864 with 100 consecutive performances of *Hamlet*, but the next year he had to shut down the Shakespeare play he was performing in because of the scandal caused by his brother's assassination of Lincoln. In February 1869, however, he opened his own theater in New York with a production of *Romeo and Juliet*. Tickets for the first performance were auctioned off at as much as $125. Although he went bankrupt in 1873 and had become even more moody and despairing than his normal nature after his brother's criminal act, Booth went on a tour of the United States and rebuilt his reputation.

Among the most popular stage performers of the period, more for their appearances and vivacious personalities than for their acting skills, were Lola Montez (1818?-1861), Ada Isaacs Menken (1835-68) and Lotta Crabtree (1847-1924). Miss Montez, who was Irish but claimed Spanish descent, achieved a reputation for flamboyant adventures before she was seen in the

United States. She was the mistress of Louis I of Bavaria but was expelled for aiding a revolution there in 1848. She opened her American tour in 1851, married a San Francisco journalist in the course of it, and challenged a Sacramento editor to a duel. Miss Montez' dancing was mediocre but her beauty and charm made her popular with male audiences. Mrs. Menken was born in Louisiana and her real name was Dolores Adios Fuertes. She became a dancer while in her teens but did not achieve the heights of her popularity until 1863, when she first appeared in *Mazeppa, or the Wild Horse*. One critic wrote of the "magnificent audacity" with which, at the climax of the play, she came on stage, wearing very little and lashed to the side of a horse. Miners especially loved this performance and in Virginia City, Nevada, they presented her with a gold bar worth $2,000. Miss Crabtree was taught to dance when she was six by the then more famous Lola Montez, and within two years she was touring the western mining camps. Although she was a hit in New York in 1867 in a dramatization of Dickens's *The Old Curiosity Shop*, her most appreciative audiences were the miners who loved her spirit, her red hair and her famous Spider Dance.

Two leading producers and theatrical managers of the period were James W. Wallack (1791-1864) and Augustin Daly (1838-99). Wallack was a British actor who came to the United States in 1852 and managed his own theater in New York until he died. He had one of the best repertory companies and his theater was noted for its elegance and dignity. When Wallack died, he was succeeded by his son, Lester (1820-88), who was also a playwright. Daly began his career as a drama critic, and in 1867 became a theatrical manager with the production of his own play *Under the Gaslight*, the kind of melodrama in which the hero is tied to the railroad tracks or otherwise placed in dire peril. He opened his own theater in 1869. One of his best plays was *Horizon*, a romantic drama of the West. Fanny Davenport (1850-98), born in London, made her stage debut in Boston in her first adult role when she was only fifteen. She joined Daly's company in 1869 and became its reigning star.

Tom Taylor (1817-80), an English dramatist who was also a professor of English in London, wrote more than 100 plays, including *The Ticket-of-Leave Man* (1863), but his best-known play in America was *Our American Cousin*, originally seen in New York in 1858. Joseph Jefferson's first success in New York came when he played in it, several years before his *Rip Van Winkle*. The British actor Edward A. Sothern (1826-81) made his name in New York as Lord Dundreary in *Our American Cousin* and, in fact, almost took over the play as he built up the character he portrayed. Laura Keene (c. 1826-73) also became closely connected with the play. She was a British actress who settled in America in 1855, and the next year became the first woman theater manager in the country. Her most famous production was *Our American Cousin* and she and her company were presenting the play at Ford's Theater in Washington the night Lincoln was assassinated. It was the kind of simple comedy that enabled Lincoln to forget for a bit the strains of being a war president.

# 17  Architecture, Science, Medicine

No LANDMARK achievements stand out in architecture, science or medicine in America during the Civil War era. Architects adapted foreign styles and the only distinctive contribution was in construction, where the innovative use of iron as a structural material was seen. Science grappled with the problems posed by the theory of evolution, but the exploits of geologists and others in exploring the Far West were more exciting.

Professionalism in architectural training and practice increased with the founding of the American Institute of Architects in 1857 and with the establishment of the first school of architecture at the Massachusetts Institute of Technology in 1866. The Greek Revival style, copied from the architecture of ancient Greece, and which had been popular for half a century, was in decline. Interest in the perpendicular, arched Gothic style of the Middle Ages began before mid-century and Gothic became a particularly popular style for churches and college buildings. At first, the Gothic style copied was that of England and France. After the war, however, taste changed and the more lavish and colorful Gothic of Venice, with colored stonework and carved colonnade arcades was favored.

Richard Upjohn (1802-78) was a pioneer architect of the Gothic revival, and set one of the best examples in his design for Trinity Church in New York, which he finished in 1846. In 1852 he published a design for a Gothic church that could be built in wood, and it was copied in hundreds of American towns and villages. After the war, a taste for elaborate, showy buildings influenced architecture. An example of this can be seen in the extravagant Gothic style of the state capitol in Hartford, Connecticut. It was designed by Upjohn's son, Richard M. Upjohn (1828-1903). With the elder Upjohn, James Renwick (1818-95) led the Gothic revival, although he later designed in other styles. Renwick was chosen as architect of St. Patrick's Cathedral in New York in 1853 and this, the largest Gothic-style church in the country, was his masterpiece. His use of the Second Empire style is shown in Charity Hospital, New York, built between 1858 and 1861.

Another architectural style of medieval Europe was introduced at this time—Romanesque, whose source was the public buildings of the Roman Empire and which matured in the eleventh century. This style gave a massive effect, featured rounded arches and a tower, or twin towers. Henry Hobson Richardson (1836-86) was the leading exponent of Romanesque in America. After studying at the Ecole des Beaux Arts in Paris, considered the foremost architectural school in Europe, Richardson began practicing in New York in 1866. His first large project, and his finest work, is Trinity Church in Boston, built between 1872 and 1877, in the French Romanesque manner. Richardson had a strong influence on American architecture throughout his career.

In the post-Civil War period, a variety of other architectural styles, or combinations of styles, came into use. None was simple and many of the buildings were exceedingly ornate, often following the whims of those who had money to spend but no knowledge of architecture. One popular style was that of the Italian villa of stone, with a flat-topped tower and arched windows.

No architectural style was more popular than that known as

Second Empire, named for the 1852 to 1870 reign of Napoleon III of France. These buildings, whether public or private, featured mansard roofs with their two slopes and dormer windows. The buildings were also lush with French Renaissance detail. In America, Second Empire became known, somewhat derisively, as the General Grant style because many Federal government buildings were built this way. The foremost example is the State, War and Navy Building (now the Executive Office Building) in Washington, designed by Alfred B. Mullett. The so-called Queen Anne style became popular in the late 1860's. It had no relation to the early eighteenth century when Queen Anne reigned in Great Britain. A Queen Anne house is a very complicated-looking structure from the outside, having no unity of design. The ground plan is irregular and various ridges and turrets intersect on the roof. Several different building materials may be used and there is much elaborate trim and paneling. At the time it was considered the most modern style one could choose.

The possession of wealth and the desire to demonstrate it inspired such homes as Olana, built for Frederick E. Church, painter of the Hudson River School, who was paid as much as $10,000 a canvas. Church acted as his own architect for this structure on a hill overlooking the Hudson, which was begun in 1870. He based the plan, in general, on Near Eastern themes, so there were many turrets, towers and gazebos. Ornamental tiles and bricks abounded. Frederick Law Olmsted landscaped the grounds. In the popular summer resort of Saratoga, New York, the United States Hotel was erected in 1875. It is described in one architectural history as "an enormous Mississippi River steamboat planted on turf." At Newport, Rhode Island, a rival of Saratoga for the patronage of rich summer residents, rather modest homes prevailed until the 1870's. Then between 1874 and 1876 Richardson designed a large house for Watts Sherman. Built of brick, stone and timber, it had sweeping roofs and tall chimneys. One French château-type house had been built in Newport earlier, and before long the town possessed a number of pseudo-Renaissance palaces.

While public buildings and private mansions received a great deal of attention from architects, little heed was paid to the design of factories—a growing part of the architectural landscape—or to housing for ordinary people. The railroad boom did create an architectural and construction need that could not be overlooked. Railroad stations succeeded churches in presenting the problem of placing roofs over very large spaces. As station sizes increased, vaulted forms had to be used instead of gabled roofs. The Philadelphia terminal of 1851-52 was a pioneer structure in using the technique of erecting a vaulted shed on timber-arched trusses. The trainshed of the Grand Central Depot (1869-71) in New York, which was 600 by 200 feet, was spanned by numerous trussed arches that made a spider web pattern.

The most significant development in building construction was the growing use of iron, not just as a design element but structurally. Prefabricated iron columns appeared in the 1850's, most copying classical and Gothic styles. James Bogardus (1800-74) and Daniel Badger, born in 1860, did more than any others to revolutionize construction by the use of iron. Bogardus took out a patent for an iron building in 1850, having already constructed a four-story factory of iron in 1848-49. Badger and Bogardus were competitors in this new business and Badger opened a foundry in New York in 1847 to produce iron fronts for buildings. The best example of the use of his materials is the five-story department store of E. V. Haughwout and Company, built in New York in 1857, where the first passenger elevator was installed. After the war, Badger supplied the iron for a six-story grain storage warehouse in Brooklyn.

The most extensive use of iron in a public building in the early 1850's occurred when two wings were added to the Capitol in Washington. Iron was used extensively in several new and larger department stores, one of its advantages being that it allowed more window space. The Lord and Taylor building on lower Broadway was described in 1859 by *The New York Times* as an "Italian palace." The iron framed, five-story building erected in 1859-60 as the new A. T. Stewart store was the largest iron building up to that time. Structural iron and passenger elevators combined to make higher office buildings practical. Such structures in New York in 1865 were four or five stories; by 1875 several were nine or ten stories high. The Equitable Life Insurance Company building of 1870, 130 feet high, demonstrated that space on the top floor could be rented profitably. Richard Morris Hunt (1829-95) designed a 230-foot high building for the New York *Tribune* in 1870. Hunt, who was the first American to study at the Ecole des Beaux Arts, later designed Newport mansions and the base for the Statue of Liberty, among other projects.

Alexander Jackson Davis (1803-92) was the most prolific architect of his day, and usually used the Greek Revival style. In 1853 he laid out one of the first planned suburbs, in West Orange, New Jersey, but it was not for the average wage earner. On a 500-acre site, he allowed five to ten acres per home and retained a park of fifty acres for the use of the owners of the houses in Llewellyn Park.

Along with Frederick Law Olmsted, Calvert Vaux (1824-95)—although he designed buildings of many different kinds, including what he hoped would be a model tenement—specialized in landscape architecture. He assisted Olmsted with the design of several parks, including Central Park, and laid out others himself. Both men favored romantic-style landscapes, whether in cities or not. Vaux, who was born in London and came to the United States in 1857, was the architect who designed the Metropolitan Museum of Art and the American Museum of Natural History.

American scientists were active in all fields of study and made varied contributions, both theoretical and practical. They could not help but get involved in the debate over Darwin's theory of evolution, and most came to accept it. Geology remained a favorite science because so much of the western United States remained to be mapped, searched for minerals and examined for its history and its features.

The leading chemist, as his father had been before him, was Benjamin Silliman, Jr. (1816-85). The school of chemistry he established in 1847, during his first years on the Yale faculty, developed into the Sheffield Scientific School. He returned to Yale in 1854 to succeed his father, after having taught at the University of Louisville since 1849. Lewis M. Rutherfurd (1816-92) practiced law for a dozen years, but then turned to physics and worked mostly in celestial photography. He invented several instruments for use in such work, including a telescope adapted for astronomical photography. Josiah Willard Gibbs (1839-1903), after studying abroad, joined the Yale faculty in 1871. He published his first two papers containing equations for the mechanical action of heat in 1873. After 1875 he produced notable work in the theory of thermodynamics and other aspects of mathematical physics. Still another Yale professor, James D. Dana (1813-95), was a leading geologist. Dana was the specialist in that field with the government's expedition of 1838-42 to the Antarctic and the South Seas. Later he wrote a number of books, including *Manual of Geology* (1862), which was the standard for many years.

Asa Gray (1810-88) began collecting and identifying plants as a boy, and in his adult years was one of the leading botanists of the century. He was professor of natural history at Harvard from 1842 to 1873, where he taught many future botanists and wrote textbooks. His *Manual of Botany*, revised many times, is still standard. Gray was a strong supporter of the theory of evolution before it was generally accepted, even by scientists.

One of Gray's Harvard colleagues, Louis Agassiz (1807-73), on the other hand, opposed Darwin even though some of his own work seemed to contain evidence supporting the British naturalist. Agassiz was born in Switzerland and came to the United States in 1846, where he taught and lectured on zoology and geology. His work, including a research expedition along the whole coast of the Atlantic and the Pacific from Boston to California, gave considerable impetus to science in his day.

John W. Draper (1811-82) was scientist, philosopher and historian combined. A chemist, he also helped found the medical school at New York University. He took up photography as soon as he heard of the process Daguerre had invented in France in 1839, and later he took the first photographs of the moon. In science, Draper's chief contribution was his research in radiant energy. Among Draper's books, *History of the Conflict between Religion and Science* (1874) was both influential and controversial. His son Henry Draper (1837-82) was a physician and professor of physiology at New York University from 1870 to 1882. His major work, though, was in astronomical photography and spectroscopy.

Lewis Henry Morgan (1818-81), a New York State lawyer by training, became interested in the Indians of his area and as a result ended up as a pioneer anthropologist and ethnologist. He was adopted by a Seneca tribe in 1847, and a book he wrote in 1851 was both the first scientific account of American Indian life and an excellent description of the society. His *Systems of Consanguinity* in 1870 was a landmark, starting the study of kinship systems. As Morgan pioneered in anthropology, so did Othniel C. Marsh (1831-99) in paleontology. He was appointed to the first chair in that subject at Yale in 1866, and he led many expeditions in the West, from Nebraska to California. The resulting collection of fossil vertebrates was the largest in the world at the time. In all, Marsh discovered 500 new species but his best-known exploit was the restoration of dinosaur skeletons.

Some of his discoveries, such as the fossils of extinct toothed birds, lent great support to Darwin.

Curiosity about the Far West and its mountains, deserts, canyons and odd geological formations was widespread, both among the general public and scientists. The Federal government sponsored a number of expeditions, usually with geologists in charge, and often including painters and photographers, to the benefit of future generations. Among the geologists who tramped over the West was Josiah D. Whitney (1819-96), who first took part in an expedition in the Lake Superior region in 1847-49. He was state geologist of California from 1860 to 1874 and directed explorations that found important mineral deposits. Mt. Whitney, the second highest peak in the United States, is named for him.

Clarence King (1842-1901), who studied under Agassiz and Whitney, persuaded Congress to support the 40th Parallel Survey, which was undertaken between 1867 and 1872 and of which he was chief geologist. The survey studied the mountain ranges running from eastern Colorado into California. King wrote the geological section of *Mining Industry* (1870), a classic in economic geology. John Wesley Powell (1834-1902), who lost his right arm fighting on the Union side at Shiloh, taught geology before leading expeditions in 1867 and 1868 in Colorado and Utah. The next year he was in charge of an expedition sponsored by the Smithsonian Institution to make a geographical and geological survey of the Colorado River. In the course of his exploration, Powell went by boat through the Grand Canyon and described his dangerous trip in a book in 1875.

Ferdinand V. Hayden (1829-87), who served in the war as a surgeon, was also interested in geology and in 1867 began various surveys in the nation's territories that went on for twelve years. His work in the Rocky Mountains was especially useful. While he was with the geological survey in Montana, he was largely responsible for the creat on of Yellowstone National

Park in 1872. Joseph Leidy (1823-91) was the nation's foremost anatomist and his textbook on human anatomy, published in 1861, was long the best in the field. He classified the fossils collected by Hayden on his expeditions and was the first to identify in the United States some extinct species of the horse, camel, sloth, tiger and rhinoceros. The Scottish-born naturalist John Muir (1838-1914) arrived in America in 1849 and as a young man studied chemistry, geology and botany. He made many journeys, mostly on foot, through several parts of the country. In 1867, for example, he started a 1,000-mile walk from Wisconsin to the Gulf of Mexico. The next year he made a trip from Indiana to the Pacific Coast, keeping a journal which was published much later. A leader in the forest conservation movement, and a crusader for national parks, Muir had much to do with the establishment of Yosemite National Park.

Neither Thomas Moran (1837-1926) nor William Henry Jackson (1834-1942) was a scientist, but they added much to the work of the geologists exploring the West. Moran accompanied both Hayden and Powell on expeditions and illustrated their reports. Later, from such sketches, he produced two large canvases in the Capitol, *The Grand Canyon of the Yellowstone* and *Chasm of the Colorado*. Jackson was both an artist and a photographer. Settling in Omaha, Nebraska, in 1868, he photographed natural and historical sites in a wide area of the West, including the building of the Union Pacific Railroad and typical mining towns. His photographs of the Yellowstone region played a part in bringing about the establishment of the national park.

Other Americans left the United States to explore the oceans and foreign lands. Among them were Elisha Kent Kane (1820-57) and Isaac Israel Hayes (1832-81). Kane was the medical officer on the first United States-Grinnell Expedition, named for Henry Grinnell, who financed it. This search party went to the Arctic region to try to find traces of the expedition led by Sir John Franklin, which had set out in 1845 and never returned.

The American group sailed in 1850 and Kane's account of it in an 1853 book was read from coast to coast. Kane was the leader of a second expedition which sailed in 1853 and set a record for reaching a point farther north than anyone had achieved before. The expedition also sighted the Humboldt Glacier and brought back new and additional knowledge of Greenland. Kane wrote an account of this journey, too, published in 1856, and he died the following year as a result of the hardships he had endured. Hayes was the medical officer of the second Grinnell expedition and in 1860-61 led one of his own which sought an open seaway to the North Pole. Hayes thought he had reached the pole, but his calculations were wrong.

Charles Francis Hall (1821-71) also became interested in the search for the Franklin expedition, and in 1860-62 explored part of Baffin Island, east of the Northwest Territories of Canada, with Eskimo companions. He found no trace of Franklin but he did come upon evidence of Martin Frobisher's expedition of almost 300 years earlier. Hall was placed in command of a government expedition in 1871 to try to reach the North Pole by ship. He set a new northern-most record but did not reach the pole. Hall died while the party was in winter quarters and most of the rest were killed on the return voyage when an ice floe smashed their ship. On the other side of the world, a naval officer, John Rodgers (1812-82), led a northern Pacific surveying and exploring expedition off the coast of China and in the Arctic from 1852-1856. Rodgers later served in the Civil War and commanded the Asiatic fleet from 1870 to 1872.

Matthew F. Maury (1806-73), a naval officer who had played a large part in the establishment and development of the Naval Observatory, was a leader in devising charts of ocean winds and currents to aid navigation. His *Physical Geography of the Sea* (1855) was the first modern text on oceanography. Maury joined the Confederate side in the war and afterward served under the Emperor Maximilian in Mexico, where he tried to found colonies of former Confederates. The publication of timely weather forecasts, made possible by the telegraph, began before 1850 and developed rapidly in the next quarter-century. Under the guidance of the Smithsonian Institution, thirty-one states had weather observers in 1854, and by 1860 there were 500 weather stations. The first to issue daily weather forecasts was Cleveland Abbe (1838-1916), a meteorologist, in about 1868, when he headed the Cincinnati Observatory. Congress established a national weather service in 1870 and placed it in the Army Signal Corps. Abbe joined the service the following year.

Although epidemics of such diseases as yellow fever and typhoid fever continued to ravage American cities and medical science had not yet pinpointed the causes of these diseases, some progress was made in public health. A *Report of the Massachusetts Sanitary Commission*, published in 1850 and written by Lemuel Shattuck (1793-1859), demonstrated the need for sewage disposal systems, but it was 1869 before a Board of Public Health was established. Even so, Massachusetts led the nation. The Federal government formed the Public Health Service in 1870 while the American Public Health Association was organized in 1872.

# 18 Education, Religion, Reform

AS IN other fields, the Civil War had disruptive effects on education, religion and reform, but Americans continued to be concerned with such matters. The abolitionists were highly vocal
and noticeable, but many men and women were active in other
reforms and in education and religion.

Except in the South, by 1860 most states had set up public
school systems, and about half the children of the nation were
receiving some education. Many schools were one-room log
structures but in another decade or so these were mostly
replaced by larger, although still one-room, frame buildings.
The winter session lasted no more than three months and
teachers were paid at most $35 a month. The South possessed
very few free public schools, but had a growing number of
private, or semiprivate academies. Since these were usually not
free, most children of poor families received no schooling at all.

Colleges increased in number and so did their student
bodies, with the South more nearly the equal of the North in
higher education than in public schools. A larger proportion of
southern young white males, in fact, went to college than did
their northern counterparts. Shortly before the war, the University of Virginia, with 606 students, had a larger enrollment than
either Harvard or Yale. Postgraduate education was in its early
days and the first doctor of philosophy degree granted in

America was given by Yale in 1861. The war disrupted education in the North to the extent that many teachers and students volunteered. In the South, however, the educational system was all but wiped out. Schoolhouses were destroyed or abandoned and a number of colleges were closed for some time during the war and Reconstruction. In that latter period, though, the new state governments in the South formally established free public school systems.

Far-reaching in its ultimate effect on education was the Morrill Land Grant Act of 1862. The law took its name from Justin S. Morrill, a founder of the Republican party who had served in the House and the Senate from Vermont for forty-four years. Morrill first introduced a bill in 1857 to give each state public lands for the support of education, but the South opposed it as contrary to states' rights and President Buchanan vetoed it. After the southern states seceded, a similar bill was passed in 1862 and was signed by President Lincoln. It gave each state 30,000 acres of land for each senator and representative. With money received from the sale of the land, each state was required to establish at least one school. These schools were to emphasize the teaching of practical matters, such as agriculture, the mechanical crafts and home economics. The bill, in part, was intended "to promote the liberal and practical education of the industrial classes in the several pursuits and professions of life." In all, 17,000,000 acres of land were allotted and eventually seventy colleges were established.

A growing number of colleges opened their doors to women during this period, while several institutions for women only were founded. Vassar College, endowed with $800,000 from Matthew Vassar (1792-1868), a successful brewer, was chartered in 1860 and opened its doors in 1865. Wellesley College, chartered in 1871 and receiving its initial class in 1875, was the first women's college to have science laboratories. Smith College, chartered in 1871 and teaching its first students in 1875, took its name from Sophia Smith (1796-1870), who endowed it. A few women took advantage of slowly increasing educational opportunities to enter professions hitherto reserved for men. Best known among such pioneers is Elizabeth Blackwell (1821-1910), the first woman in the United States to receive a medical degree, which she earned in 1849 from the Geneva Medical College. With others, she opened the New York Infirmary for Women and Children in 1857.

Higher education for blacks made some progress before the war as well as after. The oldest school whose original purpose was to provide college-level instruction for blacks was Lincoln University, in Pennsylvania, founded as the Ashmun Institute in 1854. Wilberforce University in Ohio followed in 1856. Mary Jane Patterson became the first black female in the country to graduate from college when Oberlin gave her a degree in 1862. Shortly after the war, three educational institutions to serve the freed slaves were established. The earliest was Fisk Institute, which opened in Nashville, Tennessee, in 1866 and was named for General Clinton B. Fisk, an official of the Freedmen's Bureau. Howard University in Washington, founded in 1867, took its name from General Oliver O. Howard, chief commissioner of the Freedmen's Bureau, who served as president of the new school from 1869 to 1873. Hampton Institute in Virginia began teaching students in 1868 as a result of the need for vocational and agricultural education recognized by General Samuel C. Armstrong (1839-93), who had been an agent of the Freedmen's Bureau and who was president of Hampton. This school also pioneered in educating Indian youths.

A group of distinguished educators in the postwar years introduced new ideas and new methods into American higher education. Among the older generation were Frederick A. P. Barnard (1809-89), Henry Barnard (1811-1900) and Noah Porter (1811-92). Frederick Barnard was president of the University of Mississippi from 1856 to 1861, when he went north because of the war. Named president of Columbia in 1864, he held the post until 1889, during which time he transformed the small college into a modern university. Barnard offered more elective courses and advocated equality in education for women. Henry Barnard, early in his career, was a leader in improving and reforming the public schools of the country. Later he was chancellor of the University of Wisconsin, and in 1867 became the first United States commissioner of education. In this post he led the way in gathering statistics and disseminating reports on all aspects of education. Porter, on the other hand, was more traditional. As president of Yale from 1871 to 1886, he staunchly defended Greek and Latin and rated the sciences below the humanities. Porter was a forceful foe of Darwinism, but his book *The Human Intellect* (1868) was an important early work in psychology. He also edited a revised edition of Noah Webster's standard dictionary in 1864.

Three men who more than others of their generation shaped the modern American university were Daniel Coit Gilman (1831-1908), Andrew D. White (1832-1918) and Charles W. Eliot (1834-1926). Gilman, at Yale, was instrumental in establishing the Sheffield Scientific School, after which he accepted the post of president of the new University of California. He was appointed first president of Johns Hopkins University in 1875 and spent a year organizing it and selecting an excellent faculty for what soon became an outstanding institution. White, while in the New York State legislature, worked for a land grant to set up an agricultural school. When the grant was approved, he and Ezra Cornell founded Cornell University, and White, as president from 1867 to 1885, expanded the school far beyond its original scope. He was one of the first to use the system of elective studies. Eliot met some opposition when he was named president of Harvard in 1869 because he was only thirty-five years old and was a scientist and a layman. Harvard's previous presidents had been clergymen. In the forty years he served,

Eliot made Harvard into one of the finest universities in the world. He organized graduate schools, introduced the idea of the sabbatical leave, offered elective courses, insisted on written exams and relaxed student discipline.

Edward A. Sheldon (1823-97) was an innovator in teacher training at the Oswego (New York) State Normal and Training School, where he was principal from 1862 to 1897. He was one of the first to use practice teaching. Sheldon made the school a center for spreading the ideas of Johann H. Pestalozzi (1746-1827), a Swiss educational reformer whose theories are at the foundations of modern elementary education. Pestalozzi thought teaching methods should match the natural order of the child's development. Susan Blow (1843-1916) opened the first successful American kindergarten in 1873 in St. Louis, and also a training school for kindergarten teachers. She was helped by William T. Harris (1835-1909), who was superintendent of the schools in St. Louis. Harris later served as Federal commissioner of education and was internationally known as an interpreter of German philosophical thought.

Changes and new trends appeared in the field of religion also, some brought about by the war. In the North, a gradual movement could be discerned away from the strict moral and religious code of Puritanism, partly because of the influence of transcendentalism, partly because of the acceptance of new scientific theories. The South, though, became more conservative and Puritanical in religious matters after the war. With a passionately loved cause defeated and economic life blighted, southerners turned to the comfort of the religious beliefs of earlier days.

Immigration played a part in religious movements also. Some of the more recently arrived Lutherans from Germany and Scandinavia did not like the practices of Lutherans who had arrived earlier and so organized their own groups. German-language parochial schools were established. Since all the Irish and French-Canadians and about half the Germans who emigrated to the United States were Roman Catholics, that church grew larger in proportion to others. This growth, in turn, brought an anti-Catholic reaction from Americans with an antiforeign and nativist inclination. Finally, Judaism in this quarter-century became a significant factor in American religious life, and the United States became the center of Reform Judaism in its divergence from Orthodox Judaism.

The leaders of Catholicism in America were John J. Hughes (1797-1864) and John McCloskey (1810-85). Hughes was born in Ireland, came to America in 1817 and was made bishop of New York in 1842. Eight years later, he was appointed the first American archbishop. Hughes was such an ardent defender of Catholicism that he aroused much opposition. He appeared on the scene at a time when the Catholic Church, which had hitherto avoided any display of power, had expanded so much that it became more aggressive in asserting its beliefs. Hughes, for example, delivered a sermon in the fall of 1850 in which he predicted the decline of Protestantism until the whole world was dominated by the Catholic Church. He also seems to have been behind an 1852 campaign in which Catholics were urged to demand public money for their schools, or, at least, a law against the reading of the Protestant Bible in tax-supported schools. McCloskey, Hughes's successor, was far less controversial. Born in Brooklyn, he became the first American cardinal in 1875, was the principal builder of St. Patrick's Cathedral and founded many churches and seminaries.

Anti-Catholicism took various forms, including a certain amount of violence along with wild rumors. John S. Orr, usually known as the Angel Gabriel because he wore a white robe and gathered his audience by blowing a horn, caused a riot in Boston in 1854 by his inflammatory speeches against Catholicism. Around the country in the mid-1850's about a dozen Catholic churches were burned and others damaged. Rumors swept New

England in 1855 that Irish girls in domestic service had been told to poison their Protestant employers' food.

At the same time that more Jews than before were coming to the United States from Europe, Judaism was in the throes of a debate between those who wished to retain all the rituals and practices of Orthodox Judaism and those who believed that Judaism should be modernized. The debate moved to America and here the new movement found leadership in two rabbis, David Einhorn (1809-79) and Isaac Mayer Wise (1819-1900). They had much to do with both the formulation and the organization of Reform Judaism, which brought changes in worship, in temple government and in religious education. Where Orthodox Judaism insisted on holding to the letter of the Scriptures and the Oral Laws (commentaries on the legal parts of the scriptures), Reform leaders believed the important point was the ethical content and that ritual aspects could be simplified.

Einhorn was born in Bavaria and emigrated to America to become a rabbi in Baltimore in 1855. That same year he contributed many of the ideas incorporated in a statement, adopted by a rabbinical conference, that became the basis of Reform Judaism for a generation. The original *Union Prayer Book* was modeled after his prayer book. Einhorn was forced to leave Baltimore in 1861 because of southern antagonism to his anti-slavery stand. Wise was born in Bohemia and arrived in the United States in 1846. Beginning in 1854, he was a rabbi in Cincinnati, Ohio, where he advocated adapting Judaism to American life. Wise worked for a union of Reform congregations, which came into being in 1873 as the Union of American Hebrew Congregations, and in 1875 he founded Hebrew Union College, the first institution in America to train rabbis. The ferment in Judaism also resulted in a third group, Conservative Judaism, whose religious and ritual position was between the other two. Rabbi Isaac Leeser (1806-68) and Sabato Morais (1823-97) were the Conservative leaders. The order of B'nai

B'rith, founded in 1843 to promote culture and philanthropy, did important work among the growing number of Jewish newcomers to America, especially in the cities.

A number of Protestant clergymen achieved national reputations and none was better known or more in demand as a preacher than Henry Ward Beecher (1813-87), son of Lyman Beecher and brother of Harriet Beecher Stowe. A Congregational minister, Beecher took the pulpit of a new church in Brooklyn in 1847, where his eloquence, not only on religious subjects but others, won him audiences of 2,500 people to hear his Sunday sermons. His rhetoric was sentimental and showy, but he threw all his energy into advocating such reforms as abolition (he said the Fugitive Slave Law should be disobeyed), and woman suffrage, and he supported the theory of evolution. He went to England in 1863 to defend the Union cause in public appearances. The most sensational jury trial of the period took place in 1874, when Beecher was accused by Theodore Tilton (1835-1907) of adultery with his wife. The Tiltons were members of Beecher's church and Tilton was an editor of religious magazines. The trial lasted for months, until, in 1875, the jury disagreed on a verdict and the issue was never settled. While the suit damaged Beecher's reputation, he went on with his work.

T. DeWitt Talmage (1832-1902) was a Presbyterian clergyman who, after becoming minister of a church in Brooklyn, also attracted very large congregations. His parishoners built an enormous tabernacle for him in 1870, but it burned two years later, as did two others built in the following twenty years. One held 4,600 people. Talmage had a sensational style of speaking and preached the old-fashioned, literal gospel of the Bible. He carried on a long crusade against vice in New York City, and he sometimes went on tours late at night with the police, looking for crime and sin. Although less sensational, Phillips Brooks (1835-93) was another influential preacher of the day. He was an Episcopalian and occupied the pulpit of Trinity Church, Boston, from 1869 to 1891. In the course of his career he became a bishop and he wrote the words for "O Little Town of Bethlehem."

The first woman to be ordained a clergyman in the United States was Antoinette L. Blackwell (1825-1921), who, graduating from Oberlin College in 1847, was one of the first women to receive a college education. She was ordained a Congregational minister in 1853, but later became a Unitarian. She was an active worker for women's rights, suffrage and temperance. Olympia Brown (1835-1926) graduated from theological school in 1863 and was ordained the same year. She married in 1873 but retained her own name. For thirty years head of the woman's suffrage group in Wisconsin, she joined in picketing the White House for women's rights when she was in her eighties.

Individuals and groups advocating many reforms were unusually active before the war, but as war drew nearer the abolition question overshadowed all others. The abolitionists, who in this period became more numerous and more vociferous, took up the cause for different reasons and in various ways. Most of the feeling against slavery grew out of the religious spirit of the time in which slavery was seen as a sin. Others demanded an end to the institution because it was contrary to the ideal of democracy and the equality of human beings. Some abolitionists preached, lectured, published antislavery newspapers and wrote pamphlets. Others demonstrated. Opposition to the Fugitive Slave Law brought out acts of heroism and violence in rescuing slaves, sometimes by force, while the "Underground Railroad" was an organized system for escorting slaves out of the South to free territory. Its work had been going on for some time before the war and no one knows how many slaves escaped this way. One man, Elijah Anderson, operating from Ohio and known as the "general superintendent" of the railroad, led more than 1,000 slaves to freedom by 1855. People went to prison for such efforts, one man spending fifteen years in jail in Kentucky after being caught. Another man who aided fugitive slaves and was jailed in Cincinnati was hailed as a hero and was brought fresh strawberries and other food by abolitionists.

There were many leaders among the abolitionists, including such diverse people as Gerrit Smith (1797-1887), William Lloyd Garrison (1805-79), Wendell Phillips (1811-84) and Josiah B. Grinnell (1821-91). Smith spent a good deal of his fortune on reforms and was an organizer of the Liberty party and its candidate for governor of New York in 1840. He is thought to have aided John Brown with his plans for the raid on Harpers Ferry. Garrison had been publishing the *Liberator*, the most widely known abolitionist journal, since 1831, and was president of the American Anti-Slavery Society from 1843 to 1865. A violent tempered man who advocated secession by the North, he publicly burned a copy of the Constitution on July 4, 1854. Garrison opposed the Civil War until Lincoln's Emancipation Proclamation. At the time, Garrison seemed to be the leading abolitionist, but others were more effective despite his clamor.

Phillips, a member of an old and wealthy New England family, first became an active abolitionist in 1835 and was the movement's most talented orator. He said many harsh words about Lincoln and opposed his renomination because Phillips did not think he was doing enough to end slavery. After the war, Phillips broke with Garrison, whom he had supported for many years, because Garrison felt that emancipation marked the end of the struggle. Phillips believed much more needed to be done to educate and otherwise assist the blacks. A clergyman, Grinnell created a sensation and lost his pastorate when he preached an antislavery sermon in a Washington church in 1852. It was to Grinnell that editor Horace Greeley gave his famous advice: "Go west, young man, go west." Grinnell did, and the land he gave to Iowa College in 1859 resulted in its name being changed to honor him.

During the war, a large number of women dropped their

efforts on behalf of women's rights to assist in war work. Some took over the tasks of men who had joined the armed forces, while others were busy in relief work. Many such women hoped that after the war they would be rewarded for their efforts and for, as they saw it, having shown they were men's equals. But although some progress was evident, they were disappointed when the amendments to the Constitution changing the status of blacks did not also give women the vote. A National Woman's Rights Convention was held in Worcester, Massachusetts, in October 1851, and others in later years, while the first National Woman's Suffrage Convention met in Washington early in 1869. Women were first given the vote in Wyoming Territory in 1869 and in Utah a year later. After the war, however, when Kansas held a referendum on votes for blacks and women, both lost, the women by a larger margin than the blacks.

Elizabeth Cady Stanton (1815-1902) and Susan B. Anthony (1820-1906) met in 1851, and for half a century thereafter worked together as the leaders of the women's rights movement. Mrs. Stanton was one of the organizers of the first women's rights congress in 1848, and was also an active abolitionist. She was president of the National Woman Suffrage Association from 1869, when it was founded, until 1890. Miss Anthony spoke and worked for abolition and temperance laws as well as for women's rights. When she tried to vote in 1872 as a test of the Fourteenth Amendment, she was arrested and fined, but refused to pay.

The temperance movement made considerable progress before the war. Thirteen states had prohibition laws of some kind by 1855, and by 1860 all the northern states and most of the southern ones passed such laws. Then the tide receded as laws were repealed or declared invalid by the courts. Also, as the war brought the need for more tax revenue, there was temptation to legalize liquor so it could be taxed. Frances E. Willard (1839-98), after being president of the Evanston (Illinois) College for

Ladies, in 1874 helped organize the Woman's Christian Temperance Union, of which she became president in 1879. She was also active in such causes as woman's suffrage, but she devoted most of her life to promoting temperance.

While abolition, women's rights and temperance attracted the most attention among reform movements, many other people were active in other ways that they thought would benefit the nation. Charles Loring Brace (1826-90), a pioneer in child welfare methods, founded the Children's Aid Society of New York in 1853. He wanted to move slum children out west to live a rural life but later saw this was impractical. Brace also wrote a number of books, including *Short Sermons to Newsboys* (1866). Henry Berg (1811-88), a New York philanthropist, founded the American Society for the Prevention of Cruelty to Animals in 1866, the first organization of its kind in the United States. Nine years later, he was one of the founders of the American Society for the Prevention of Cruelty to Children.

# 19 Life in America

IN SPITE of the Civil War and Reconstruction, many aspects of life went on much as before: fashions changed, new entertainment and entertainers caught the public fancy, new sports were introduced and men and women made news for both good and bad deeds.

More substantial and ornate houses were built and furnished, partly as a result of increasing national wealth, partly because machinery now produced furniture, textiles and ceramics more cheaply than before. At the same time, though, these factory-made goods became more elaborate in design and displaced handcrafted articles. The taste of the period turned toward the heavy and cluttered effect in home furnishings, beloved in the Victorian era, named for Great Britain's somber Queen Victoria. In the North, in the 1860's, frame dwellings replaced many of the earlier farmers' log cabins, but farms still lacked most conveniences. Bathrooms were not yet common in many places and a well-appointed bedroom had a water pitcher, a wash bowl and a covered slop basin. Tin bathtubs were brought out for use on Saturday night. A Yale student in 1858 noted he was happy to find his boardinghouse had a bathroom, while Vassar College, as soon as it opened, required its students to bathe twice weekly.

A large part of the population grew some or all of its own food, but city dwellers, especially the working class, had to worry both about prices and about the condition of food when it reached the city. *Harper's Weekly* commented in 1869 that "the city people are in constant danger of buying unwholesome meat." Ice was used by some to preserve food, and a Boston family could be supplied for the summer at $2 a month. Typical prices around 1850 included beef at 10 cents a pound; flour, $5 a barrel; sugar, 8 cents a pound; butter, 32.5 cents a pound; and a bushel of potatoes, $1.

Women of the 1850's looked to Paris for fashion trends, and after the Empress Eugenie was married to Napoleon III in 1853, the styles she wore were widely copied. This was the period of the hoopskirt, which ballooned out from a woman's waist and was exceedingly awkward for getting through doors or into carriages. Around 1870, the bustle, a horsehair pad or wire cage worn in the back under a woman's skirt, became the fashion. With it went very long, elaborate dresses with puffed out upper sleeves. Also, as part of the Victorian manner, women wore tight corsets of steel and whalebone so that a young woman's waist might be constricted to no more than fifteen inches. Although the long cutaway coat of the 1850's went out of fashion, men for the most part wore black suits, white shirts and black stocks. Young dandies wore more colorful clothes and even some businessmen wore white linen or seersucker in the summer, but no man would be seen without a collar, cravat and waistcoat no matter what the temperature. Beards came into popularity before the war, and scarcely a picture exists of a general on either side without a full complement of whiskers.

Women were as restricted in their activities as in their clothes. By and large, society believed woman's place was in the home, where she should be an example of piety, purity, submissiveness and domesticity. In *The American Woman's Home* (1869), Harriet Beecher Stowe and her sister, Catherine Beecher, extolled women when they wrote that "no statesman . . . had more frequent calls for wisdom, firmness, tact, discrimination, prudence, and versatility of talent" than a woman in charge of a large household. Many women, of course, did work outside the home: in factories, in domestic service, as teachers, as actresses, in reform movements and, very rarely, in some "male" occupation such as stagecoach driver. They were not, however, admitted to such fields as law or business at the higher levels.

Somewhat of an exception were two sisters, Victoria Claflin Woodhull (1838-1927) and Tennessee Claflin (1846-1923). Known for many years for their beauty and their eccentric behavior, they had given spiritualist demonstrations when they were children. Cornelius Vanderbilt, who was interested in spiritualism, financed a brokerage house for them in 1866 and four years later they became publishers of a sensational journal that mingled scandal with support of reform movements. Victoria became the first woman candidate for president in 1872, when she ran as the People's party candidate.

In journalism the tradition of strong-minded editors who owned their own papers and whose opinions were apparent on nearly every page continued, with Horace Greeley the best known of all. Greeley founded the New York *Tribune* in 1841 as a paper for the working class, appealing to their interests and edited to assist them. The *Tribune* by 1860 was strongly antislavery and its weekly edition, with a circulation of 200,000 all over the North and West, was more influential than any other paper. After the war, Greeley supported Negro suffrage and amnesty for southern leaders. Charles A. Dana (1819-97) worked on Greeley's *Tribune* for fifteen years beginning in 1847 but he left when his views on the war were too militaristic for Greeley. He became editor and part owner of the New York *Sun* in 1868, and the well-written *Sun*, with Dana's admonition "be interesting," became known as "the newspaperman's newspaper." Dana fought editorially the corruption of the Grant administration.

Henry J. Raymond (1820-69) also worked for Greeley and

was influential in New York State politics in the 1840's. He founded *The New York Times* in 1851, and through the paper helped launch the Republican party. Raymond was determined to publish a paper that was less biased and more impartial than the other papers of the day. Oldest of the leading editors was James Gordon Bennett (1795-1872), a Scotsman, who founded the New York *Herald* in 1835 as a paper to sell for only a penny. He was one of the first to use the telegraph extensively for gathering news and his coverage of the Civil War, with sixty-three correspondents, constituted excellent journalism.

A number of magazines were launched. The *Atlantic* (1857) was the organ of the dominating New England intellectuals, while *Harper's New Monthly Magazine* (1850), which had Henry Raymond as its first editor, reached a circulation of 200,000 in two years. *Harper's Weekly* (1857) achieved its readership chiefly because of its coverage, with illustrations, of the Civil War. New journals designed for women were *Harper's Bazaar* (1867) and *Woman's Home Companion* (1873). Two magazine editors who were examples of the popular and the intellectual were Frank Leslie (1821-80) and Edwin L. Godkin (1831-1902), the former born in England, the latter in Ireland. Leslie established *Frank Leslie's Illustrated Newspaper* in 1855 and achieved both attention and profit during the war when, using new techniques, he was able to get into print quickly the exciting illustrations his artists sent from the battlefields. Godkin, who established the *Nation* in 1865, edited a magazine of comment and opinion on public affairs which had substantial influence. The magazine's literary style was distinguished and it advocated such measures as civil service reform.

The "dime novel" appeared on the scene and captured millions of readers. The first such adventure story that sold for ten cents was *Malaeska, the Indian Wife of the White Hunter* (1860) by Ann S. Stephens, the sales of which reached 300,000 copies in the first year. The leading publisher of dime novels was Erastus

Beadle (1821-94), who sold over 4,000,000 copies during the war, many to soldiers. Most dime novels were set in the Revolution, the Civil War or on the frontier. One of the most prolific of dime novel authors was E. Z. C. Judson (1823-86), who wrote under the name Ned Buntline, and turned out more than 400 such stories. Judson was an adventurer, a trapper and an accused murderer who had served time in jail. He gave William F. Cody the name "Buffalo Bill," and wrote a series of dime novels in which he was the hero.

Netta Victoria Victor (1831-86), whose husband Orville James Victor (1827-1910) was Beadle's editor, wrote *Alice Wilde, the Raftsman's Daughter* in 1860. It was the fourth in Beadle's series and concerned a sophisticated New Yorker who goes to the frontier and falls in love with the daughter of a raftsman. Another early and prolific dime novel author was Edward S. Ellis (1840-1916), who turned from school teaching to write *Seth Jones; or, The Captives of the Frontier* in 1860. This story, which sold 450,000 copies in six months, used the device of a disguised hero whose true identity is revealed only at the end. Under various names Prentiss Ingraham (1843-1904), after serving in the Civil War, wrote more than 600 dime novels. *The Masked Spy* (1872) was the first and about 200 in all dealt with Buffalo Bill. One series of tales was devoted to Deadwood Dick, whose real name was Richard E. Clarke (1845-1930). Born in England, he became an Indian fighter and guard for gold shipments in South Dakota. Although he is sometimes thought to be the author of the books about him, they were actually written by Edward L. Wheeler.

The performing arts offered a variety of entertainment, from singers to musical shows to daredevils. Jenny Lind (1820-87), a Swedish coloratura soprano with a voice of excellent quality, was a sensation wherever she went on her tour of the United States in 1850-52, which was sponsored by the showman Phineas T. Barnum, and made them both much money. Charles

Dickens, the most popular novelist of the time, came to the United States in 1867-68 and gave readings from his own works to rapt audiences in a number of cities.

A new kind of stage production, combining melodrama and ballet in a lavish production, was a hit in New York in 1866. This first long-running musical show on Broadway, *The Black Crook*, gave 474 performances and was considered immoral by some because of its fifty lightly clad dancing girls. Two years later, *British Blondes* was even more daring when imported from England and was more like the modern burlesque show than anything seen before. It played around the country for twenty years. Other shows that entertained audiences included Swiss bell ringers, a reformed gambler who did card tricks and a steam calliope drawn by forty horses. Large theaters were built, the Hippodrome in New York, which opened in 1853, seated 4,600 and offered chariot races as well as clowns and acrobats. On the Mississippi and Ohio rivers, showboats brought glamor to small towns along the banks, although the palatial passenger steamers on the same rivers were infested with an estimated 2,000 professional gamblers in the 1850's.

Tony Pastor (1837-1908), on the stage as a dancer and singer from boyhood, began, in 1861, to turn the variety theater, which had a reputation for vulgarity, into family entertainment. He opened his own theater in 1866, and by offering door prizes such as kitchen ware and dress patterns, attracted women patrons as well as men. Pastor became the "father of American vaudeville." Charles Blondin, a French acrobat, crossed over Niagara Falls on a tightrope in 1859, and a few days later did it blindfolded while pushing a wheelbarrow. The nation had a world's fair to attend in 1853, when the Crystal Palace was opened in New York City. A building of iron and glass, its dome was 148 feet high, while more than an acre of glass went into its construction. Displays showed the latest advances in industry and technology, but the building burned down in 1858.

Two frontiersmen whose exaggerated exploits made them popular heroes for many years were William F. ("Buffalo Bill") Cody (1846-1917) and James Butler ("Wild Bill") Hickok (1837-76). Buffalo Bill began to earn the family's living when he was only twelve, after his father's death. By 1859 he was in the Colorado gold fields and the next year rode for the Pony Express. He was also a buffalo hunter for railroad construction crews. Ned Buntline, the dime novelist, talked Cody into appearing on the stage in 1872, playing himself, and thereafter, except for a brief spell of scouting against the Sioux in 1876, Buffalo Bill was in show business with a thrilling "wild west" show. Wild Bill Hickok took part in the struggle over slavery in Kansas and was a Union scout in the war. Later he was a United States marshall in several towns, including Abilene. Wild Bill built up a reputation as a marksman and for engaging in desperate encounters with outlaws. After going on the stage with Buffalo Bill in 1872-73, he moved to Deadwood, South Dakota, where he was murdered a few years later.

The traveling circus developed into a super-spectacle with two or more rings and sideshows of freaks and curiosities beginning about 1870. Phineas T. Barnum (1810-91), who organized a circus in 1871, already had an international reputation for his American Museum in New York City, which, for many years, had drawn crowds to see its freaks and oddities, some fakes. His primary attraction was Tom Thumb (real name: Charles Sherwood Stratton, 1839-83), a midget who never grew taller than thirty-three inches. After he married Lavinia Warren, a dwarf, in a fashionable wedding in 1863, the newlyweds were received at the White House by President Lincoln. Barnum, whose first big circus attraction was Jumbo, a six-and-a-half-ton elephant, in 1881 merged his show with that of James A. Bailey, who had started a circus in 1873.

Americans enjoyed a variety of simple amusements, from picnics to trips to amusement parks such as the Elysian Fields in

Hoboken, New Jersey. Holidays were particular days for cele-
bration. Independence Day, of course, was the biggest holiday,
with parades which always included war veterans. There was
much oratory and firing of cannons, rifles and revolvers.
Thanksgiving Day had been celebrated by the Pilgrims and a day
of such observance was proclaimed in 1789 by President
Washington. The custom had died out but was revived in 1863
by Lincoln at the urging of Sarah J. Hale, editor of a woman's
magazine. Memorial Day was first observed in 1868, when
Union General John A. Logan, head of the veterans organization, the Grand Army of the Republic, set it aside to decorate the
graves of Civil War veterans. Within ten years, veterans of the
North and the South held joint ceremonies in honor of those
who died in the conflict.

The war brought forth many songs, but the most popular,
both North and South, seems to have been "When This Cruel
War Is Over." The South adopted "Dixie," written in 1860 for a
minstrel show, and "The Bonnie Blue Flag" (1862) as its favorite
marching songs. The most impressive and lasting of the war
songs was "The Battle Hymn of the Republic," written in 1861 by
Julia Ward Howe (1819-1910) and sung to the music of "Glory,
Glory, Hallelujah." Mrs. Howe, who later was elected the first
woman member of the American Academy of Arts and Letters,
received $4 from the *Atlantic* for her verses. She was the wife of
Samuel Gridley Howe (1801-76) and they were both active in the
abolition movement and other reforms. George Root (1820-95),
one of the most successful song writers of the time, contributed
"The Battle Cry of Freedom" and "Just Before the Battle,
Mother" in 1863 and "Tramp, Tramp, Tramp" in 1864. Henry
Clay Work (1832-84), inspired by General Sherman, wrote
"Marching Through Georgia" in 1865, but the general thought
it gave too much importance to the event. Work also wrote
"Father, Dear Father, Come Home with Me Now" and
"Grandfather's Clock," both very popular in their day. Conduc-

tor Patrick S. Gilmore contributed "When Johnny Comes Marching Home" in 1863.

Stephen C. Foster (1826-64) was the most prolific and popular song writer of the period. Among his compositions were "Camptown Races" (1851), "My Old Kentucky Home" (1853), "Jeannie with the Light Brown Hair" (1854) and "Old Black Joe" (1860), as well as the war song "We Are Coming, Father Abraham, 300,000 More" (1862). When he died in poverty at the age of thirty-seven, a few cents and the manuscript of "Beautiful Dreamer" were found in his pocket. Foster's knowledge of Negro music came to him only through minstrel shows, but because the songs seemed authentic to listeners, they were thought of by many people as being true folk music. Many other songs that were sung for several generations appeared: "Darling Nelly Gray" (1856), "Jingle Bells" (1857), "When You and I Were Young, Maggie" (1866) and "Silver Threads Among the Gold" (1873). Fanny Crosby (1820-1915), accidentally blinded in infancy, wrote the words for hundreds of hymns, such as "Blessed Assurance," sometimes turning out half a dozen a day.

Until the 1860's very few organized sports existed and few people, except children, played outdoor games. As more people had leisure time and as somewhat fewer used all their energy in work, a change came about. Roller skating grew quickly in popularity among young and old after a practical four-wheel skate became available in 1863. Three years later, a public skating rink was opened in Newport, Rhode Island, and before long, a larger one for 1,000 skaters opened in Chicago. Croquet was introduced from England and became a fashionable game, one that women could play as a part of their social life. It was so popular that one manufacturer offered a set with candle sockets on top of the wickets for playing after dark. In 1874, tennis was also imported from England, and Newport and New York became the centers of this sport. The game as played then, with the ball hit gently back and forth over a high net, allowed women to participate even though they had to hold up their long, dragging skirts with one hand.

Rowing as a competitive sport went back to the early years of the century, but the first intercollegiate race did not take place until 1852, when Harvard and Yale met. Twenty years later, the first regatta for amateurs was staged in Philadelphia. Horse racing was an even older sport, but the first thoroughbred racing took place at fashionable Saratoga Springs, New York, in 1863, and the first Kentucky Derby at Louisville, Kentucky, was run in 1875 with a horse named Aristides the winner. Harness racing, with pacers and trotters, was popular in the 1870's.

Boxing was considered vulgar and was illegal in many places, but championship bouts drew fans from all walks of life. The American champion, John Heenan (1835-73), went to England to meet the British champion, Tom Sayers (1826-65), in 1860. After a bare-knuckled, forty-two round fight that lasted two hours and twenty minutes, the fight was declared a draw when the crowd invaded the ring. Both fighters were considerably battered. Heenan lost his title in 1863.

Football, played more or less like the modern game, was introduced to the nation by the colleges beginning in 1869, when Princeton and Rutgers met, with twenty-five men on a side and Princeton won, six goals to four. The next year, Rutgers beat Columbia, six to three, and in 1872 both Harvard and Yale took up the game.

Baseball began in the second quarter of the century and by the 1850's was well on the way to becoming the national sport. New York and Brooklyn each had four clubs in 1854 and Chicago the same number four years later. The first club on the Pacific Coast was organized in 1859. As many as 2,000 people paid fifty cents each to see a game in 1858, apparently the first time admission was charged. The Excelsiors of Brooklyn toured four states in 1860, and at home against the rival Atlantics drew a crowd of 15,000. The war slowed the spread of baseball to some extent but the game became popular in army camps and so farm and small-town children were introduced to it. The start of professionalism in baseball came in 1866 with the organization of a national association of 202 clubs. The first fully professional team was the Cincinnati Red Stockings of 1869, which didn't lose a game all summer. The manager was Harry Wright (1835-95), an Englishman who switched from cricket to baseball and became the "father" of the professional game. The National Association of Professional Baseball Players was organized in 1871 and its first pennant was taken by the Philadelphia Athletics.

Among people of accomplishment or in the public eye—or both—were a photographer, a lithograph publisher, a society leader, a journalist-adventurer, a train robber, a European revolutionary and one of the first environmentalists. Matthew B. Brady (c. 1823-96) was an early photographer who opened his studio in New York in 1844 and was very successful. He took his first photograph of Lincoln in 1860 and later received permission to follow the armies with his camera. He employed a staff of twenty and spent $100,000 covering the war, compiling an invaluable photographic record of the conflict, but the effort cost him his health and his fortune. Nathaniel Currier (1813-88), who took James Merritt Ives into partnership in 1857, produced lithographs by the thousands on every conceivable subject of American life, and made them popular in almost every household.

Ward McAllister (1827-95) came from Georgia to New York and in 1853 married a millionaire's daughter. In a few years he was the social arbiter of society in New York and Newport. McAllister selected twenty-five men from leading New York families in 1872 to be, as he called them, "patriarchs," who would set the tone for society. Two Astors were included, as well as representatives of old Dutch families. Henry Morton Stanley (1841-1904), a British-born adventurer, came to the United

States in 1857. While fighting for the Confederates at the battle of Shiloh he was captured by the North, after which he served for a while in the Union navy. When the Scottish missionary David Livingstone (1813-73) was reported missing in Africa, the New York *Herald* commissioned Stanley to go look for him. He found his man in November 1871, and greeted him with the still-famous words: "Dr. Livingstone, I presume."

Jesse James (1847-82) at the age of fifteen joined a Confederate guerilla outfit, and in 1866, with his brother Frank (1844-1915) formed an outlaw gang. They robbed banks at first but about 1873 they began to specialize in holding up trains. Jesse was eventually killed by one of his own gang, but Frank lived on respectably as a farmer. The Hungarian patriot Louis Kossuth (1802-94), who had headed the short-lived government of an independent Hungary in 1849, came to the United States in 1851, arriving on a United States Navy warship. He was received with great enthusiasm as a fighter for liberty, but Catholics such as Bishop Hughes, who called him a "humbug," did not like him because he represented Protestantism against the Catholicism of the Austrian Empire from which he had sought to free Hungary. When he began to solicit money and other support for renewing the struggle in Europe, he lost favor with many Americans who feared this would embroil the country in European affairs. The enthusiastic crowds disappeared and Kossuth left the country without fanfare. Lawyer, linguistic scholar and diplomat, George Perkins Marsh (1801-82) was also a pioneer in conservation and in warning of the danger already done to the environment. His book, *Man and Nature*, published in 1864 and revised under another title ten years later, was an attempt to show what man could and should do to restore the animal and vegetable life he had disturbed.

The thirty-seven states of the restored Union (Nevada was admitted in 1864 and Nebraska in 1867) had a population in

1870, according to the census, of 38,558,371. The next census in 1880 showed a further growth of more than 11,500,000, so that by the end of three-quarters of the nineteenth century, the population was in the neighborhood of 44,000,000, nearly double that of 1850.

The war settled some matters once and for all. The United States was one nation and the Federal government was superior to the states. Both constitutionally and practically, the argument over states' rights was dead. The West came out of the war feeling more important as a result of its contributions, and it resented the East's attitude of superiority. The South, of course, mourned its lost cause. Business and industry eclipsed politics as the main concern of the country and exercised more power in the nation's affairs. The various sections were brought together by economic forces as business and labor began to think in national terms and as factory-produced goods spread uniformity. In addition, faster systems of transportation and communication did much to blend the people and their customs over the continental expanse. Many more problems would arise— including race relations—but slavery was ended and the nation was one again.

# Reading List

AARON, DANIEL. *The Unwritten War; American Writers and the Civil War.* New York: Alfred A. Knopf, Inc., 1973.

BARTLETT, RICHARD A. *The New Country: A Social History of the American Frontier, 1776-1890.* New York: Oxford University Press, Inc., 1974.

BERGMAN, PETER M. *The Chronological History of the Negro in America.* New York: New American Library, Inc., 1969.

BOARDMAN, FON W., JR. *America and the Gilded Age, 1876-1900.* New York: Henry Z. Walck, Inc., 1972.

———. *America and the Jacksonian Era, 1825-1850.* New York: Henry Z. Walck, Inc., 1975.

BOORSTIN, DANIEL J. *The Americans: The Democratic Experience.* New York: Random House, Inc., 1973.

BRANDON, WILLIAM. *The American Heritage Book of Indians.* New York: American Heritage Publishing Co., Inc., 1961.

BURCHARD, JOHN, and BUSH-BROWN, ALBERT. *The Architecture of America: A Social and Cultural History.* Abridged ed. Boston: Little, Brown & Co., 1967.

CASH, W. J. *The Mind of the South.* New York: Alfred A. Knopf, Inc., 1941.

CATTON, BRUCE. *The American Heritage Short History of the Civil War.* New York: American Heritage Publishing Co., Inc., 1960.

———. *The Coming Fury.* New York: Doubleday & Co., Inc., 1961.

————. *Glory Road*. New York: Doubleday & Co., Inc., 1952.

————. *Mr. Lincoln's Army*. New York: Doubleday & Co., Inc., 1951.

————. *A Stillness at Appomattox*. New York: Doubleday & Co., Inc., 1953.

————. *This Hallowed Ground: The Story of the Union Side of the Civil War*. New York: Doubleday & Co., Inc. 1956.

————. *U. S. Grant and the American Military Tradition*. Boston: Little, Brown & Co., 1954.

CRAVEN, AVERY. *The Coming of the Civil War*. 2nd ed. New York: Charles Scribner's Sons, 1957.

————. *The Growth of Southern Nationalism, 1848-1861*. Baton Rouge: Louisiana State University Press, 1953.

CUNLIFFE, MARCUS. *The Literature of the United States*. Baltimore: Penguin Books, 1961.

CURRENT, RICHARD N. *The Lincoln Nobody Knows*. New York: Hill and Wang, 1958.

CURTI, MERLE. *The Growth of American Thought*. 3rd ed. New York: Harper & Row, Publishers, 1964.

DONALD, DAVID. *Lincoln Reconsidered; Essays on the Civil War Era*. New York: Alfred A. Knopf, Inc., 1956.

————. (ed.). *Why the North Won the Civil War*. Baton Rouge: Louisiana State University Press, 1960.

DULLES, FOSTER RHEA. *A History of Recreation: America Learns to Play*. 2nd ed. New York: Appleton-Century-Crofts, 1965.

————. *Labor in America*. 3rd ed. New York: Thomas Y. Crowell Co., 1966.

DUMMOND, DWIGHT LOWELL. *Antislavery: The Crusade for Freedom in America*. Ann Arbor: University of Michigan Press, 1961.

FARB, PETER. *Man's Rise to Civilization as Shown by the Indians of North America from Primeval Times to the Coming of the Industrial State*. New York: E. P. Dutton & Co., 1968.

FAULKNER, HAROLD U. *American Economic History*. 8th ed. New York: Harper & Row, Publishers, 1960.

FILLER, LOUIS. *The Crusade Against Slavery, 1830-1860*. New York: Harper & Row, Publishers, 1960.

FOGEL, ROBERT WILLIAM, and ENGERMAN, STANLEY L. *Time on the Cross; The Economics of American Negro Slavery*. Boston: Little, Brown & Co., 1974.

FRANKLIN, JOHN HOPE. *From Slavery to Freedom: A History of Negro Americans*. 3rd ed. Alfred A. Knopf, Inc., 1967.

———. *Reconstruction after the Civil War*. Chicago: University of Chicago Press, 1961.

GATES, PAUL W. *Agriculture and the Civil War*. New York: Alfred A. Knopf, Inc., 1965.

GENOVESE, EUGENE D. *Roll, Jordan, Roll; The World the Slaves Made*. New York: Pantheon Books, Inc., 1974.

GREEN, CONSTANCE McLAUGHLIN. *The Rise of Urban America*. New York: Harper & Row, Publishers, 1965.

HAGAN, WILLIAM T. *American Indians*. Chicago: University of Chicago Press, 1961.

JONES, MALDWYN ALLEN. *American Immigration*. Chicago: University of Chicago Press, 1960.

JOSEPHY, ALVIN M., JR. *The Indian Heritage of America*. New York: Alfred A. Knopf, Inc., 1968.

LEECH, MARGARET. *Reveille in Washington, 1860-65*. New York: Harper & Bros., 1941.

LEWIS, OSCAR. *The Big Four: The Story of Huntington, Stanford, Hopkins and Crocker, and of the Building of the Central Pacific*. New York: Alfred A. Knopf, Inc., 1938.

———. *Silver Kings: The Lives and Times of Mackay, Fair, Flood, and O'Brien, Lords of the Nevada Comstock Lode*. New York: Alfred A. Knopf, Inc., 1947.

MAYER, GEORGE H. *The Republican Party, 1854-1964*. 2nd ed. New York: Oxford University Press, Inc., 1967.

MIERS, EARL SCHENCK. *Robert E. Lee*. New York: Alfred A. Knopf, Inc., 1956.

NEVINS, ALLAN. *Ordeal of the Union; Selected Chapters*. New York: Charles Scribner's Sons, 1971.

NICHOLS, ROY FRANKLIN. *The Disruption of American Democracy.* New York: The Macmillan Co., 1948.

PHILLIPS, ULRICH BONNELL. *American Negro Slavery.* New York: D. Appleton & Co., 1918.

RANDALL, J. G., and DONALD, DAVID. *The Civil War and Reconstruction.* 2nd ed., rev. Lexington: D. C. Heath & Co., 1969.

SABLOSKY, IRVING. *American Music.* Chicago: University of Chicago Press, 1969.

SANDBURG, CARL. *Abraham Lincoln; The Prairie Years and the War Years.* 3 vol. ed. New York: Harcourt Brace Jovanovich, Inc., 1967.

SCHMITT, MARTIN F., and BROWN, DEE. *The Settlers' West.* New York: Charles Scribner's Sons, 1955.

SHAARA, MICHAEL. *The Killer Angels.* New York: David McKay Co., Inc., 1974.

SINCLAIR, ANDREW. *The Better Half: The Emancipation of the American Woman.* New York: Harper & Row, Publishers, 1965.

STAMPP, KENNETH M. *The Era of Reconstruction, 1865-1877.* New York: Alfred A. Knopf, Inc., 1965.

———. *The Peculiar Institution: Slavery in the Ante-Bellum South.* New York: Alfred A. Knopf, Inc., 1956.

———. (ed.). *The Causes of the Civil War.* Englewood Cliffs: Prentice-Hall, Inc., 1965.

STOVER, JOHN F. *American Railroads.* Chicago: University of Chicago Press, 1961.

THOMAS, BENJAMIN P. *Abraham Lincoln: A Biography.* New York: Alfred A. Knopf, Inc., 1952.

WASHBURN, WILCOMB E. *The Indian in America.* New York: Harper & Row, Publishers, 1975.

WEBB, WALTER PRESCOTT. *The Great Plains.* Boston: Ginn & Co., 1931.

# Index

Abbe, Cleveland, 179
abolition; *see* antislavery movement
Adams, Charles Francis, 67
Adams, Charles Francis, Jr., 137
Adams, William Taylor, 157
Agassiz, Louis, 175, 176
agriculture, 93-100, 117, 119, 130
*Alabama* Claims, 59-60, 67, 87-88, 91
Alaska, 85
Albert, Prince, 67
Alcott, Louisa May, 157
Alger, Horatio, 157
American Anti-Slavery Society, 189
American Indians, 15, 20, 102, 103, 104-110, 142, 154, 175, 196
American party, 18, 19, 25, 118
Ames, Oakes, 89
Anderson, Elijah, 188
Anderson, Robert, 33
Andersonville prison, 60, 72
Anthony, Susan B., 190
Antietam, 48, 70
Anti-Masonic party, 19
antislavery movement, 1-4, 15-16, 23, 70, 152, 153, 162, 187, 188-89, 199
Apache Indians, 106-7
Appomattox Court House, 58
Arapaho Indians, 102
architecture, 169-73
Armour, Philip D., 123

Armstrong, Samuel C., 182
Arp, Bill, 156
art, 159-62, 177
Arthur, Timothy Shay, 158
Atlanta, 55-56, 73

Babcock, Orville E., 88, 91
Badger, Daniel, 172
Baker, George F., 132
Bancroft, Hubert Howe, 153-54
banking, 38, 77, 126, 131, 135
Barnard, Frederick A. P., 182-83
Barnard, Henry, 182, 183
Barnum, Phineas T., 196, 198
Barton, Clara, 72
Beadle, Erastus, 195-96
Beauregard, Pierre G. T., 41, 44
Beecher, Catherine, 193
Beecher, Henry Ward, 187
Beecher, Lyman, 152, 187
Belknap, William W., 105-6
Bell, John, 25, 27-28
Belmont, August, 132
Benjamin, Judah P., 32
Bennett, James Gordon, 195
Berg, Henry, 191
Bessemer, Sir Henry, 121
Bierstadt, Albert, 160
Billings, Josh, 156
bison, 104, 109, 160, 198
Black Codes, 78-79
Black Friday, 133

*209*